IBD'S 10 SECRETS

Investor's Business Daily has spent ye
successful people in all walks of life. N
when combined, can turn dreams into ....y. Each day, we
highlight one.

1 **HOW YOU THINK IS EVERYTHING:** Always be positive. Think success, not failure. Beware of a negative environment.

2 **DECIDE UPON YOUR TRUE DREAMS AND GOALS:** Write down your specific goals and develop a plan to reach them.

3 **TAKE ACTION:** Goals are nothing without action. Don't be afraid to get started. Just do it.

4 **NEVER STOP LEARNING:** Go back to school or read books. Get training and acquire skills.

5 **BE PERSISTENT AND WORK HARD:** Success is a marathon, not a sprint. Never give up.

6 **LEARN TO ANALYZE DETAILS:** Get all the facts, all the input. Learn from your mistakes.

7 **FOCUS YOUR TIME AND MONEY:** Don't let other people or things distract you.

8 **DON'T BE AFRAID TO INNOVATE; BE DIFFERENT:** Following the herd is a sure way to mediocrity.

9 **DEAL AND COMMUNICATE WITH PEOPLE EFFECTIVELY:** No person is an island. Learn to understand and motivate others.

10 **BE HONEST AND DEPENDABLE; TAKE RESPONSIBILITY:** Otherwise, Nos. 1-9 won't matter.

What *Investor's Business Daily* Readers Have to Say About the "Leaders & Success" Section

I like "Leaders & Success" — I actually get my 14-year-old son to read it. I cut out the ones that I think he can relate to. He's real receptive and reads them. They're helpful because it's not just me telling him how to do something, but it's in black and white and he can read it from somebody else.

— Alan Weiss

I love how they profile successful people every day. I love the "Leaders & Success" (section). I love to read who is the leader, what did he go through to become successful. And every one of them went through tremendous character-building experiences, but instead of . . . packing up and running, they learned through those down times. They became stronger because of it.

— Mike Johnson

I find the "Leaders & Success" series to be very informative. (It) helps me in keeping an open mind to new and different ideas, thinking positive, and (realizing) that success does not usually happen by accident . . . one can be successful if he/she follows a certain general and basic approach.

— Jahandar Kakvand

I enjoy the "Leaders & Success" section. Many profiles have kept me motivated. IBD's 10 Secrets to Success is something I live by and realize how true to life they really can be as I witness my own goals becoming reality.

— John Boik

Sports Leaders
& Success

Sports Leaders & Success

55 Top Sports Leaders & How They Achieved Greatness

Introduction by William J. O'Neil

McGraw-Hill

New York   Chicago   San Francisco   Lisbon   London
Madrid   Mexico City   Milan   New Delhi   San Juan
Seoul   Singapore   Sydney   Toronto

Copyright© 2004 by William J. O'Neil. All rights reserved. Printed in the United States of America. Except as permitted under the United States Copyright Act of 1976, no part of this publication may be reproduced or distributed in any form or by any means, or stored in a data-base or retrieval system, without the prior written permission of the publisher.

6 7 8 9 0   DOC/DOC   0 9

ISBN 0-07-144101-8

McGraw-Hill books are available at special quantity discounts to use as premiums and sales promotions, or for use in corporate training programs. For more information, please write to the Director of Special Sales, Professional Publishing, McGraw-Hill, Two Penn Plaza, New York, NY 10121-2298. Or contact your local bookstore.

Library of Congress Cataloging-in-Publication Data

Sports leaders & success : 55 top sports leaders & how they achieve greatness / with an introduction by William J. O'Neil.
    p.   cm.
Includes index.
    ISBN 0-07-144101-8 (alk. paper)
    1. Athletes—Biography.   2. Athletes—Rating of.   3. Success.
I. Title: Sports leaders and success.   II. Investor's business daily.
   GV697.A1S645 2004
   796'.092'2—dc22
                                       2004005286

Contents

Introduction

Top leaders everywhere have a great deal in common — they work hard, they're driven to achieve, they're fiercely determined and they also have a singular approach that sets them apart from the competition.

How do these people get there? *Investor's Business Daily*'s "Leaders and Success" section gives you the details. By learning exactly how these people became successful, you'll be able to apply their tips, traits and experiences to your life.

In this collection of *Sports Leaders & Success*, you'll discover how Muhammad Ali used his wits and will to get his shot at the heavyweight boxing title and how he used his years of practice and training to win the fight. Learn how Ironwoman Paula Newby-Fraser turns off all mental distractions and negative thoughts that prevent her from doing — and winning — the job at hand. Rediscover how Green Bay Packers coach Vince Lombardi earned his place among the greatest of the greats and won the first Super Bowl by pushing himself and his players to the limit. Find out how No. 1 ranked golfer Tiger Woods was playing great golf by age 6 because he learned to master his concentration and strive for the perfect game. And learn how soccer superstar Mia Hamm led her teams to championship after championship by deciding early in her career to settle for nothing less than being the best.

Among the many characteristics of successful greats is their resolve to work harder and longer to reach the top of their game. No matter how often they get knocked down along the way — or how far they fall — they get up and keep trying. This is the character of champions who, once having reached their goal, keep challenging themselves to greater heights.

This was the case for basketball legend Michael Jordan. Cut from the varsity basketball team in his sophomore year of high school, Jordan didn't let it get him down. He worked hard on the junior varsity squad, putting in countless hours to improve his game. The next year, he made varsity. That drive to learn and improve himself defined Jordan's career, pushing him through several disappointing seasons with the Chicago Bulls until he finally led his team to the first of six NBA championships.

Like Jordan, baseball pitcher Nolan Ryan displayed an incredible work ethic when perfecting his game. Though his professional career got off to a shaky start — he was traded at age 25 — Ryan didn't give up. He sought others' advice for ways to improve. And, as Jordan would later do, he began a rigorous weight-training program that went against the conventional wisdom of the day. At an age when most players have long since retired, Ryan was still pitching no-hitters well into his 40s.

And guess how Wayne Gretzky developed his arguably greatest hockey skill — the ability to anticipate the puck's movement? With nothing less than countless hours of training. During summers and holidays, before and after school, on and off the ice, Gretzky used every spare moment he had to take his game to ever-higher levels, turning pro at age 17. The result? Gretzy, also called "The Great One," is considered the No. 1 player in the history of hockey.

The greatest athletes are talented, of course, but the best of all time generally reach that status by outworking everyone else of equal or greater talent. And that's a powerful lesson for us all.

In these next pages, you'll learn more lessons from the greatest athletes and coaches ever to enter the competitive arena. We hope you'll discover why we've been writing about these inspiring people for years. Every last one of their stories contains the seeds of experience and knowledge for future greatness. May their spirit and example fuel your own success story.

Acknowledgments

I'm very good at picking people who know what they're talking about, selecting which of their advice is most helpful for me and incorporating that into my psyche or my game.

— MARTINA NAVRATILOVA

It goes without saying that teamwork, hard work and dedication are the important instruments of most successful endeavors. With that said, many thanks must go out to the people who contributed their time and talents to the completion of this book. In particular, Sally Doyle, Sue Frazer, Cynthia Martin, Ken Shreve, Chris Gessel, Bucky Fox, Monica Showalter, Paul Whitfield and Susan Warfel of *Investor's Business Daily*, and Donya Dickerson and Jane Palmieri of McGraw-Hill, for their attentive guidance and thoughtful contributions to this inspirational book. And I would especially like to thank Sharon Brooks, Shana Smith and Joannè von Alroth for their insightful, tenacious and superb editorial guidance.

William J. O'Neil
Founder of *Investor's Business Daily*

PART 1

Insisting On The Best

We're going to relentlessly chase perfection. We won't catch it, but if we constantly chase it, we'll achieve excellence.

— VINCE LOMBARDI

1

Baseball Player
Willie Mays

He Gave Every Game His All
And Became A Legend

At 20 years of age, Willie Mays was in the major leagues — and feeling completely overwhelmed.

In May 1951 the New York Giants promoted Mays from the minors. He told Giants manager Leo Durocher that he didn't think he was ready to hit big-league pitching. Durocher thought otherwise and made Mays his center fielder.

But after his first 26 at bats, Mays had only one hit. He became so discouraged he was crying when Durocher found him in the locker room after a game.

"I said to Leo that he'd better 'send me back to the minors because I don't think I can hit up here. I think you brought me up (from the minors) too early,'" recalled Mays in a 2000 interview.

Durocher knew he had to get Mays to stop pressing and just play. He demonstrated to Mays the confidence he had in him. "As long as I'm the manager, Willie, you're going to play center field," Durocher told Mays. "You are the best ballplayer I have ever seen."

"Those few words that Leo said made me realize that I could play major-league ball," Mays said. "'You will be my center fielder.' That relaxed me."

Mays pounded out nine hits in his next 24 at bats. He went on to become the National League Rookie of the Year in 1951. By the end of his career, he'd slugged 660 home runs (the third-best career total ever) and 3,283 base hits. Mays was elected to the Baseball Hall of Fame in 1979, and he was named to Major League Baseball's All-Century Team in 1999.

"He's the greatest player any of us has ever seen," Durocher wrote in his 1975 autobiography, "Nice Guys Finish Last."

Steady As He Goes

Mays focused on being consistent. "I just went out there every day and did a good job, and I did it daily, not once a week. I felt by doing it daily that would make me a great ballplayer," Mays said.

"He didn't let sickness or injuries stop him. (Mays) came to the park every day to put on the uniform and play," Durocher said.

Mays was born in 1931 in Westfield, Ala., where the work ethic was instilled in him by his father, a steelworker and semipro baseball player who wanted better for his son than he had for himself.

"He didn't want me working in the mills. 'You won't make (enough) money there,'" Mays remembered his father telling him.

"What my father bestowed on me was honesty, being fair with people and making sure whatever I did, I tried to be the best at it," Mays said.

Mays' father never pushed young Willie into baseball. But once Willie showed an interest, his father saw his great ability and encouraged him.

Mays was a five-tool player. He could hit, hit with power, run, throw and field.

"My father explained to me that in order to be a professional ballplayer for a long time, you had to do all of these things very well," Mays said. "I tried to be the best in each category. In order to get to the top in baseball or anything, you have to do more than one thing well."

Mays polished his skills by taking advice from the best players when he was starting out. "I learned base running from Jackie Robinson," Mays said. Mays became an expert base runner and base stealer. He led the National League in stolen bases four straight years, from 1956 to 1959.

"I learned by taking little pieces from all avenues and (then I) fit them into my style of playing," Mays said.

After his Rookie of the Year season in 1951, Mays spent most of the 1952 and all of the 1953 seasons in the Army. He returned to baseball with a bang in 1954, winning the National League's Most Valuable Player award. But he still worked to get better. He played winter ball in Puerto Rico, where he tutored Roberto Clemente before Clemente was a major leaguer.

"Professional ballplayers never stop practicing the game. When I was named the MVP in 1954 and 1965, I still found many things I could improve on," Mays said in "Play Ball," which he wrote with Maxine Berger.

One For The Team

Mays set an example for his teammates with his trademark aggressive, all-out play. "I didn't know any other way than to play hard," he said.

He helped teach younger teammates all facets of the game, and his positive, optimistic attitude inspired them. Mays was named the first black captain in the major leagues.

Mays tailored his skills to do whatever was best for the team. In 1954, Mays was chasing Babe Ruth's then single-season home-run record of 60. Mays had 36 home runs after 99 games, when Durocher made a startling request.

"I want you to stop hitting home runs," Durocher told Mays.

The Giants were two games out of first place. Durocher saw that most of Mays' home runs were coming with the bases empty because nobody was getting on base consistently in front of Mays. By aiming for base hits, Mays could still drive in runs, but he'd also be on base more. This allowed Mays to use his speed to create more scoring opportunities for the hitters behind him.

Mays started hitting the ball to all fields instead of pulling everything to left field in the hope of hitting home runs. He hit only five more home runs the rest of the year — but raised his batting average from .316 to .345 and won the National League batting crown. The Giants won the pennant and went on to defeat the powerful Cleveland Indians in the World Series.

"Winning the pennant was more important than anything I could accomplish individually. I wasn't thinking about breaking any records. I never played baseball for records," Mays said.

Mays was an aggressive outfielder. "You must go after every batted ball with everything you've got," he wrote.

Take the 1954 World Series against Cleveland. In the first game, the Indians had runners on first and second with nobody out in the top of the eighth inning. The score was 2–2 when Indian first baseman Vic Wertz hit a shot to the mammoth center field in New York's Polo Grounds.

Mays raced back and made an incredible over-the-shoulder catch, ending up with his back to home plate, 450 feet away. He pivoted and in one motion threw to second base. The runner at second tagged up and moved to third, but Mays kept the runner on first from advancing into scoring position. The Giants got out of the inning and went on to win the game, 5–2.

"You have to think about what you're going to do before the pitch is ever thrown. You can't wait until the ball is in the air to decide. I knew exactly what I was going to do if I caught the ball," Mays said. "You have to think all plays out before they ever happen."

Mays studied opposing pitchers and kept mental notes on them. "Batting starts before the game," Mays said. "You have to know the pitcher."

"Mays knew how pitchers were going to go after him, and consequently he was always ready for them," said former Giants manager Bill Rigney, who was Mays' manager from 1958 to 1960.

To maximize his physical gifts, Mays took good care of himself. He ate right and didn't smoke or drink. "I never allowed myself to get out of shape," Mays said. "In baseball, you have to be very disciplined as far as knowing what to do and how to do it. You have to be prepared at all times."

2

Mia Hamm Set High Goals
Sure-Footed Competitor Gave America A Leg Up On The Soccer Field

The defining moment in Mia Hamm's career came not on the soccer field but across a desk.

On the other side of it was her University of North Carolina soccer coach, Anson Dorrance, who was also the coach of the U.S. women's team. He had a simple question for the sophomore: What were her goals for the upcoming season?

The competitive fire that had fueled Hamm's athletic pursuits from the time she was a girl competing with boys in everything from baseball to football showed itself.

"Much to my surprise, I blurted, 'To be the best,'" Hamm said in "The Right Words at the Right Time" by Marlo Thomas.

From Dorrance, Hamm — women's soccer's all-time scorer — learned how to go about achieving her goal. "It's about commitment, plain and simple. But saying you want to be at the very top of your field and doing it are two different things," Hamm said.

"Saying it is exhilarating and a little bit scary because you are making a choice to stand out from the crowd; doing it is incredibly hard work. You can't ever live with 'good enough.' Sometimes deciding to be the best feels great. Sometimes it's discouraging, and almost always it's exhausting. The bottom line is, if I don't go into it every day consistently committed, I won't get results."

Goal Setter

To reach the top, Hamm, born in 1972 in Chapel Hill, N.C., set up a plan of action. She combined an intense focus ("Intensity is what sets winners apart," she said) with a mental toughness, diligent physical training, proper adherence to diet and, most important to Hamm, a commitment to put her team before herself.

"I believe setting goals genuinely helps a person's growth and success; otherwise how can you really be sure what you are training for, why you're asking so much of yourself? Most people have a vague idea in their mind about the future, and that uncertainty impedes their ability to achieve greatness. Write your goals down or articulate them. This process will give you focus. Dreams without follow-through are just that — dreams," Hamm wrote in "Go for the Goal: A Champion's Guide to Winning in Soccer and Life," with Aaron Heifetz.

Sports Illustrated has called Hamm "the first female team-sport superstar" in history. She was named the National College Player of the Year three straight times (1992–94) and was the first three-time U.S. Soccer Federation Female Athlete of the Year (1994–96). She was the recipient of ESPN's Espy award for Female Athlete of the Year in 1998 and 1999.

Yet it isn't the individual awards that mean the most to Hamm; it's those she achieved with her teammates. "Our success is as a team, not me as an individual," she said. "Selflessness is a key ingredient for a winning team." And there's been much collective success. Hamm has helped lead her college and U.S. national and Olympic teams to eight championships, including a gold medal at the 1996 Olympics.

"I couldn't have scored one goal without my teammates. I love them and always will," she wrote. Hamm believes that teamwork extends beyond the actual competition to all facets of preparation.

"It is the responsibility of (all) teammates to nurture (each other) through competition. Their intensity and determination set the tone of (the) training environment. Do these players create an atmosphere that will help me improve? Do I push them every day? Do the coaches push us? Everyone plays a unique role in building a team that reaches for excellence," Hamm said.

Having reached the top individually and with her team, Hamm guards fiercely against the complacency that being a champion can bring on. "Never let yourself get too comfortable or confident, because that's when a weaker opponent can sneak up and knock you off your perch," Hamm said. "Once you have achieved something, you realize you're capable of doing it again. But each time, you must work harder because the old saying is true: It is more difficult to stay on top than to get there."

As part of her mental preparation, Hamm made a study of other great soccer players, and calls that "the best way to improve your game without actually playing." She looks for ways to further improve by watching videos of herself in action and learning every aspect of the game.

"The most important attribute a soccer player must have is mental toughness. Before you can win, you must have the will to prepare to win," Hamm said.

"Mia understands the game so well, how to make subtle passes and turn average opportunities into great chances," said teammate Brandi Chastain.

The joy Hamm displays on the soccer field is another important ingredient in her recipe for success.

"Once you experience success — and you will if you put in the work — you shouldn't be afraid to celebrate it. Unless you feel good about what you do every day, you won't do it with much conviction or passion. So celebrate what you've accomplished, but also raise the bar a little higher each time you succeed," Hamm said.

"And yet individual heroics should never overshadow the pride you take in your team. Scoring three goals in a losing effort is no occasion to turn cartwheels. You must live and die with your team. If you see a team where every player has this attitude, you will see a team of winners."

The Golden Rule

While Hamm admits to being "addicted to winning," she lives by the code of sportsmanship. Emotions can run over in athletic competition, but she still abides by the Golden Rule. "Treating people as you would want to be treated is a good rule to live by, especially in the heat of battle," she said.

"Let me tell you now that all those lessons I've shared — work harder than anyone else, be a team player, celebrate your victories —

will pay off whether or not you ever win a medal, Olympic or otherwise. If you go for the goal, like we do on the national team, you'll always be reaching for a higher place. Each victory is great in and of itself, but champions are on a never-ending quest," she wrote.

While Hamm has reached her goal of being the best in the eyes of the press and public, she still strives to be worthy of the accolade.

"Many people say I'm the best women's soccer player in the world," she said. "I don't think so. And because of that, someday I just might be."

3

Basketball Champ
Kareem Abdul-Jabbar
Determination Helped Him
Shoot Straight Up

When Lewis Alcindor first picked up a basketball as a small child, he didn't have the upper-body strength to sink a basket.

He didn't let that deter him. Once he decided that he wanted to play, he put everything into making himself the best he could possibly be.

It didn't hurt that Alcindor — who changed his name to Kareem Abdul-Jabbar when he professed Islam after college — was already 5-foot-8 in the fifth grade. But by relying on discipline, the scrawny boy would become the 7-foot-2 man some have called one of the greatest basketball players ever.

Abdul-Jabbar, who was born in 1947 in New York City, was known for trying his best. And he wasn't afraid to lose. "You won't win until you learn how to lose. . . . No one makes it without stumbling," he said.

He was a quick study — by the time Abdul-Jabbar entered professional basketball, he'd led his high school and college teams to championships and posted just six losses.

When he retired in 1989, Abdul-Jabbar held records in nine National Basketball Association categories: points scored (38,387), seasons played (20), playoff points scored (5,762), Most Valuable Player awards (six), minutes played (57,446), games played (1,560), field goals made and attempted (15,837 of 28,307) and blocked shots (3,189).

He also helped the Los Angeles Lakers win five NBA titles, and helped the Milwaukee Bucks to one. He was the NBA Rookie of the Year in 1970. He was elected to the Hall of Fame in 1995.

Bolstering Strengths

How did he become such a power in the NBA?

Before Abdul-Jabbar, basketball had been ruled by players' physical strength. Although tall, Abdul-Jabbar wasn't as tough as some other players. He knew he needed to focus on his strengths to stand out.

Abdul-Jabbar decided to bolster his approach to the game — in addition to countless hours of practice, he began to beef up his mental fitness.

While the other players talked or goofed around in the locker room before a game, Abdul-Jabbar would sit quietly reading a book. It might be on any of a variety of topics. Then he'd try to reflect on what he'd read.

He also sought spiritual inspiration, praying and thinking about his faith. He figured that if he felt peaceful, his playing would improve.

"Don't ever forget that you play with your soul as well as your body," he said in his autobiography "Kareem."

Practicing by himself, Abdul-Jabbar developed his noted "skyhook," a hook shot released as he leaped to a towering height. To make sure the shot was perfect every time, he went over it hundreds of times a day, even after he had it down pat.

The skyhook became his trademark shot and one of his most feared weapons. If the opposing team wouldn't let him get near the basket or even get set for a shot, he'd focus and just hit the skyhook. It was impossible to defend against.

Abdul-Jabbar wasn't an ace at all parts of the game, however. To strengthen his weak spots, he'd force himself to practice constantly on them. He'd focus on the fundamentals — dribbling, shooting, rebounding — to support his trickier maneuvers. These sessions both improved the execution of his shots and refined his concentration.

"(The fundamentals) may just be little things, but usually they make the difference between winning and losing," he said.

When he had a problem, Abdul-Jabbar sought advice from the experts. Take his experience playing basketball for the University of California, Los Angeles. He'd get so frustrated by a referee's bad call or a teammate's mistake that he'd stumble or miss a shot.

He asked his college coach, John Wooden, what he was doing wrong. Wooden told him he needed to learn to play without emotion. If he allowed emotion into the equation, emotion would take over and win, Wooden told him.

Abdul-Jabbar then directed himself to concentrate only on his goal — winning. He stopped reacting and paid more attention to strategy and his shooting. He started playing better than ever.

He was constantly ready to innovate. Abdul-Jabbar found that other players' fingers and elbows were catching him too often in the eyes during heavy-contact games. He knew that wasn't going to change.

So he went out and had a pair of safety goggles made to protect his eyes. Some players laughed, but Abdul-Jabbar paid no attention. He could now head right into a fray and grab the ball while others were struggling to see.

When he retired at 42, he was years older than the other NBA players. Yet he never allowed age to slow down his conditioning. "Make concessions to age, and age will take over."

To stay in peak condition, he watched his diet carefully and practiced basketball daily. He studied others fitness routines and then crafted one to suit his own needs.

Following advice from Wooden, Abdul-Jabbar shunned heavy weightlifting and concentrated on cardiovascular conditioning to capitalize more on the fast-break game he wanted to play.

Later, after he met legendary martial artist Bruce Lee, Abdul-Jabbar realized that weight training might help fine-tune his game. He added it to his conditioning program and saw his strength increase and his game improve.

Advance Man

He tried to prepare for each season well in advance. That way, when the season started he'd be ready for any challenge he faced during an actual game. In addition to training physically, Abdul-Jabbar visualized what he'd do on the court. He told himself he wouldn't just contribute to the game, he'd dominate it.

Although the center of much media hype, Abdul-Jabbar tried to deflect his celebrity. He chose to keep himself focused on the team. He didn't want to hog the ball or attention.

For instance, when opponents couldn't match him on the court with a single player — which was often — they'd shift their defense and cover him with two or three players. He knew he could devastate the opponents by himself. But he was more than willing to pass the ball to one of his open teammates.

He was so willing to share the ball that his number of assists is among the tops in the NBA.

"You can't win if you don't play as a unit," he said. "One man can be a crucial ingredient on a team, but one man cannot make a team."

This approach won him strong support from the rest of the team — allowing him to achieve his top rank.

4

Tennis Champ
John McEnroe

His Commitment To Perfection
Helped Him Win Big

John McEnroe liked things to be perfectly on the mark. But that desire was hurting his record.

McEnroe was playing junior tennis. Unlike Wimbledon or the U.S. Open, there ordinarily aren't any officials to call the lines. Players have to ask for a linesman if they want one.

Therein lay McEnroe's problem — he never made such a request. He was scrupulously honest and assumed everyone else would be, too.

A tournament official once told his father, John Sr., that whenever a shot was close to the line, McEnroe called the point against himself. He felt it was his duty to own up to his mistakes.

That painstaking commitment to perfection allowed McEnroe to climb to the top of tennis. He gathered 77 singles championships, including seven Grand Slam titles, and 77 more in men's doubles, including nine Grand Slam wins. He became the youngest man to reach the Wimbledon finals at age 18, and was an invaluable member of the American Davis Cup team for eight consecutive years.

Hooked As Youngster

McEnroe strove to be the best in tennis. From the time his parents sent him to his first tennis lessons when he was 8, he knew that playing the sport was what he wanted to do.

He played well from the beginning, and he set his sights on conquering the tennis world.

To make sure he was well-known for his skill, he played as many tournaments as he could. He insisted on following the rules strictly and refused to compromise. When someone tried to bend the rules, he never hesitated to point it out.

At first, people misinterpreted his outspokenness when he thought others weren't as committed to the game. But McEnroe refused to accept substandard play or rulings.

Gradually, fans came to realize he gave his very best every time out. Born in 1959, he went to the semifinals in mixed doubles for 1999's Wimbledon at an age when many pro tennis players have retired. (He had to default when his partner, Steffi Graf, had to withdraw.) He's also active on the senior circuit.

McEnroe knows that fans expect him to be outspoken. He gives them what they want; while he no longer shouts or screams, he isn't shy on the court.

Even in exhibition games, McEnroe keeps his focus on winning. "I haven't figured out how to enjoy losing," he told *Sports Illustrated* magazine. "As you get older, the pain of losing gets greater."

Top players such as McEnroe earn a great deal of money each year in exhibition matches. Unlike some pro athletes, though, McEnroe remains devoted to the purity of competition: He plays only those matches that provide a real challenge.

For example, he refused to play a lucrative series of exhibition matches in one of South Africa's supposedly independent black republics before apartheid ended because he felt the series was an excuse for a showcase, not a real match.

"I don't like the idea of being used to show off a supposedly black state that appears to exist at the convenience of the South African government," he said.

When he does play in an exhibition, he has so much respect for the fans — and the game of tennis — that he plays as hard as he would at a major tournament.

Take the time he played an exhibition match against archrival Jimmy Connors. It was an unseasonably cold night, and the Connors-McEnroe match was the final one on what had been a good evening of tennis.

When Connors quickly and easily won the first set, restless fans expected McEnroe to tank the last set and head for the exit. But McEnroe knew the fans had paid to see a good match. He wouldn't quit.

He played his hardest for the full three sets. His effort paid off, and he won, returning to his hotel exhausted at 2 a.m. His biographer, British tennis journalist Richard Evans, asked him why he did that.

"I know exhibition matches like this offer a great opportunity to practice relaxing on court, maybe even to have a bit of fun," McEnroe said. "But I just can't let go."

Seeks The Utmost

McEnroe demands the best from himself — and those around him. When they don't give it, he finds a way to urge them to try harder.

In another exhibition match, this one against Ivan Lendl, McEnroe felt his opponent wasn't giving his all. He decided to try to motivate Lendl.

"I know that 90% of the other players would just have taken a 6–1, 6–1 victory and gone away, but I just took that — Lendl's coasting — as a total insult to the game of tennis," he told *Sport* magazine. "So I just started getting all over him on the changeovers, (and he yelled) back at me, 'You cannot say that to me.'"

The strategy worked.

"Of course, what I ended up doing was getting him to try harder than he ever tried in his life," McEnroe recalled.

Despite his numerous successes, McEnroe keeps his life in perspective. He tries to stay humble and lead a low-key life with his children. Although he realizes he's a good tennis player, he said he was uncomfortable when *Newsweek* magazine put him on its cover. "I'm not a president or something," he told biographer Evans.

When the *Daily Telegraph of London* pressed him about his numerous achievements, he conceded he'd won big tournaments but added, "It's only tennis. What I do as a human being is much more important."

That's the reason McEnroe doesn't hold grudges. For example, at one tournament he got into a screaming match with Boris Becker.

After cooling down, he realized that his behavior was rude and insulting. The next day he invited Becker to dinner.

"We needed to talk things out," McEnroe said. "I (wanted) to get it out in the open and put it behind us."

Straightforward Attitude

That attitude has endeared him to his peers and fans, if not the tennis establishment. He's been a big supporter of the U.S. Davis Cup team and holds numerous Davis Cup records, including years played (13) and singles matches won (41).

He's lobbied to become the team captain, but he's too often been too critical of the program to win the post. Still, it's important to speak up, he says.

"I don't like being a phony; I prefer to be honest," McEnroe said. "I think that's more important than being liked by everybody."

That same no-nonsense, speak-your-mind attitude has stayed with him in his post-tour life. He's a commentator for the USA Cable Network and for NBC.

He also briefly ran an art gallery in New York City's Greenwich Village. McEnroe discovered that in the art world, as in the tennis world, quality wins out. He purchased a Renoir landscape for $300,000 but traded it in relatively quickly.

"It was a Grade B piece," he told *Sports Illustrated,* "and I've learned you've got to get the best."

5

Football Coach
Paul "Bear" Bryant
Determination Drove Him And
His Players To Victory

Paul "Bear" Bryant was trying to be patient while rebuilding Texas A&M's football program in the 1955 season.

But he figured he shouldn't have to endure losing while doing it.

Bryant (1913–83) had swiftly turned around football programs at the universities of Maryland and Kentucky before taking over the struggling Texas A&M program in 1954. Bryant's first Texas A&M team posted only one win and nine losses. It would be the only losing season in his 38-year coaching career.

In the first game of the next season, Texas A&M suffered the disappointment of a 21–0 loss to the powerful University of California, Los Angeles, team.

Bryant decided right then that he needed to reach his players' pride. He gathered them in the locker room before their second game.

He asked his players to look in the mirror before they took the field. Then he said, "When you come back in here tonight, you're going to look in it again. You'll have to decide then if you gave your best. And every morning you shave from now on you're going to think about giving your best . . . because I'm going to remind you," Bryant recalled in his autobiography "Bear," written with John Underwood.

Bryant's team went out and beat Louisiana State 28–0. With his team more experienced and upgraded in talent because of his first recruiting class, Bryant's approach put the team over the top for the season. Texas A&M went on to finish with a 7-2-1 record.

"Motivating people (is) the ingredient that separates winners from losers — in football, in anything," Bryant wrote.

"Coach Bryant doesn't coach football. He coaches people. . . . The feeling was he could get more out of people than anybody," said Bum Phillips, a Bryant assistant coach who later became a National Football League head coach.

Bryant's style wasn't "rah rah" or constant yelling.

"Coach Bryant had an aura about him. He was an expert on what he did. I used to hear him (say) all the time that there was no substitute for knowledge," said former NFL and Alabama head coach Gene Stallings, who both played and coached under Bryant.

Bryant focused on motivating not only players but also his coaching staff and himself. He was born in rural Moro Bottom, Ark., the 11th of 12 children, and he'd seen the hard times of farm life. His drive to be a successful football coach came out of "that fear of going back to plowing and driving those mules and chopping cotton for 50 cents a day," he wrote.

Bryant's coaching career started in 1945 and ended in 1982. His 323 career victories rank first all-time among Division 1-A (major college) football coaches. He produced six national championship teams, all at Alabama, which had won only four games in the three years before Bryant's arrival in 1958. Bryant was elected to the College Football Hall of Fame in 1986.

Plain Old Hard Work

As the years went by, Bryant changed some things, but his fundamentals stayed the same. "You're still going to win with preparation and dedication and plain old desire," Bryant said in 1974.

While playing football at Alabama, Bryant made the decision he wanted not only to be a head coach but "a great head coach," he wrote. He believed there were no shortcuts to success.

As a young coach at Kentucky, "I was determined I was going to outwork everybody, and I worked day and night, talking with people, sitting home hours by myself working on things," Bryant wrote.

He set the example for his coaches and players.

"If (my assistant) coaches were due at 5:30 (a.m.), I got there at 5," Bryant wrote. He also "never asked anything of my players I wouldn't do myself or hadn't done at one time or another."

Bryant said he tried to be as close to his players as he could without destroying the delicate coach-player relationship.

"I love my players," Bryant wrote, "love them as if they were my own."

His rules for them were few and simple: "I expect them to act like gentlemen: to be punctual, to be prayerful. I expect them to be up on their studies."

Bryant let nothing stand in the way of his principles. When he suspended his star quarterback, Joe Namath, who was a junior, for the last two games of the 1963 season for breaking training, he wasn't sure he could win. He followed through on the suspension anyway.

Alabama won its last two games, including the Sugar Bowl.

Namath said later that he learned from his mistake and was grateful to Bryant. So was another Alabama and future NFL star quarterback, Ken Stabler, after he was suspended for a time for letting his grades slip.

"(Bryant) taught me discipline," Stabler said, "that there's a responsibility to others. . . . He wanted to teach me a lesson that would stay with me for a long time, and it has."

Bryant developed three coaching rules for winning. First, he surrounded himself with assistants and players who shared his passion, people "who can't live without football."

His second rule: "Be able to recognize winners. They come in all forms."

Third, Bryant said, have a plan for everything and stick to it. "(Have) a plan for practice, a plan for the game, a plan for being ahead and a plan for being behind 20–0 at the half."

"Coach Bryant had a burning desire to win. Some people are just satisfied being so-so. He wasn't," Stallings said.

Everyone Contributes

Bryant gave his assistant coaches autonomy and encouraged their suggestions, provided they followed his edict: "I don't want ideas just thrown out; I want them thought out," he said.

He accepted full responsibility for his football program and freely admitted his mistakes to the team.

"His philosophy as far as players were concerned is that if the team was successful they did it, and if for some reason we lost, he took the blame for it," Stallings said.

The way Bryant treated players and coaches earned him their loyalty. "Everybody wanted to please him," Stallings said.

To gain an edge in recruiting Alabama's best high school players, Bryant made allies of state high school coaches by holding highly informative coaching clinics. He soon began getting his share of the best players.

Bryant's practices were a model of efficiency. "We had people come from all over the country to watch our practices from an organizational standpoint," Stabler recalled.

"We stressed conditioning," Bryant wrote, "believing that a better-conditioned athlete can whip a superior athlete who isn't in top shape. If my 75% (player) plays 15% over his ability and your 100% (player) slogs around and plays 15% under his, then we will beat you every time."

After Alabama slipped to consecutive 6-5 records in 1969 and 1970, Bryant showed he wasn't too set in his ways to make a major change. In 1971, he installed a running offense known as the "Wishbone T."

To prepare, Bryant had spent time learning it from then-University of Texas coach Darrell Royal. With the wishbone in place, Alabama went 11-1 in 1971 and then compiled a 113-16-1 record during the remainder of Bryant's tenure. He won three more national championships with it — in 1973, 1978 and 1979.

Even with such success, Bryant never lost his focus on the players.

"Formations don't win football games; people do. But (formations) can give you an edge, and that's what coaches look for," he said.

Bryant was fond of a plaque he had that read "Winning Isn't Everything, But It Beats Anything That Comes In Second."

"That sounds a little stern to some people," Bryant wrote, "but when you're committed to a winning effort, there's nothing more gratifying in the world."

6

Soccer Superstar Pelé
He Became The Game's Greatest
By Never Letting
His Enthusiasm Flag

Edson Arantes do Nascimento was so poor as a child he used a sock stuffed with rags as a soccer ball. When he could find a grapefruit, he used that instead. He didn't get his first cleats until he was 12 years old.

But poverty didn't stop Edson, better known as Pelé, from becoming the greatest soccer player in the world. He practiced until he was the best. Pelé's scoring record is an unsurpassed 1,281 goals in 1,363 professional games — a lifetime average of 0.94 goals per game over a 21-year career that ended in 1977. He's also the only player to have won three World Cups — in 1958, 1962 and 1970 — as a member of the Brazilian team.

Growing up, he had few choices other than soccer.

"As a child, I also wanted to become a pilot," Pelé told Peter Bodo and David Hirshey in "Pelé's New World." "A child cannot go into the airplane to practice, but he can live in the street and play football, so I forgot about the airplanes."

Between school and shining shoes at night, he played soccer as often as he could when he was growing up in the small Brazilian town of Bauru.

Equal Footing

Pelé's first coach was his father. He taught him how to pass and head the ball properly and how to kick the ball with either foot. Developing the skills to score goals equally well with his head or either foot was key to his success.

"If you ever want to be a decent player, you have to learn to use each foot equally without stopping to think about it," Pelé recalled in "My Life and the Beautiful Game," written with Robert L. Fish.

Of course, Pelé — born in 1940 — was more than a strong player physically. He mastered the mental side of soccer as well, learning to outsmart defenses and psych out opposing goalies.

Pelé played soccer the way some people play poker. He was a master bluffer. He never telegraphed a kick or pass with extra body movements that could tip off goalies and defending players as to what he was going to do.

"The thing I admired the most is that when he released the ball you never knew if he was going to release it, pass it, shoot it or cross it. He would be running, and suddenly the ball would be gone," said Ron Newman, a coach of the Kansas City Wizards professional soccer team and a former player. Newman coached the Dallas Tornado when Pelé was on the New York Cosmos from 1975 to 1977 in the North American Soccer League.

The ball, Newman said, "seemed to come away from his body without any body movement, such as moving the shoulders, so other players couldn't anticipate his move. I encourage my players to do that."

Pelé also used training to overcome the limitations of his relatively short 5-foot-8 frame. Through practice he learned to jump as high as much taller players.

His biggest influence was Valdemar de Brito, a member of the 1934 Brazilian World Cup team, who picked 13-year-old Pelé for a junior team. De Brito's ingenious exercises taught Pelé to master the game's essential moves.

"For heading the ball, he had three balls hung up high above our heads, and we would have to run and jump up to hit the ball with our foreheads," Pelé told Fish.

Since Pelé was the shortest player on the team, he had to jump higher to reach them. He credited the exercise for conditioning him to leap much higher than most of his peers.

Pelé never stopped studying his sport. When he played his first game for the Cosmos in 1975, he missed three shots in the first half. He noticed that the U.S. soccer balls were lighter and softer than Brazilian ones, which was throwing off his game.

"If you hit (the ball) as hard as you do in Brazil, it's going to go off on an angle, and take off over the bar. It will take some time, but I'll get my kicks adjusted to the ball," he told reporters after the game. And he did.

Rapid Response

De Brito's training exercises simulated game conditions. One involved spreading all the team players in a circle and sending one player to the center. The player in the center would try to take the ball away from his teammates as they passed or headed it quickly between each other.

"It developed rapid reactions, and in a short time we were prepared to receive the ball without warning and pass it off, all in a split second," Pelé said.

He always kept intense enthusiasm for the sport. Late in his career, while playing for the Cosmos, Pelé complained about an NASL rule requiring shootouts to decide tie games. A shootout pits one player at a time against a goalie. The team that scores the most goals after five kicks apiece wins the game.

It's not that Pelé was bad at shootouts. He was the best shooter in the league. But as Cosmos teammate Rick Davis recalled, "I've never known anyone who has had the passion, the love and respect for the game that he has. And things like shootouts take away from the beautiful game in his eyes."

7

Heroic Life Of
Ted Williams

Baseball's Last .400 Hitter
Swung For Perfection

Ted Williams wanted to be the best. But not just by a technicality.

Heading into the last day of the 1941 season, Williams' batting average stood at .39955. Statistically, that rounded off to .400. With his Boston Red Sox already eliminated from the pennant race, Williams' manager, Joe Cronin, offered to sit him out of the season-ending doubleheader against the Philadelphia Athletics to protect his average.

"I told Cronin I didn't want that. If I couldn't hit .400 all the way, I didn't deserve it," Williams wrote in "My Turn at Bat: The Story of My Life," with John Underwood.

Williams (1918–2002) pounded out six hits in the doubleheader and finished the season at .406. He remains Major League Baseball's last .400 hitter.

To bat .400 was his longtime dream. Plus this: "I wanted to be the greatest hitter who ever lived," Williams said. "A man has to have goals — for a day, for a lifetime — and that was mine, to have people say, 'There goes Ted Williams, the greatest hitter who ever lived.'"

That's what many people said during his life and in the wake of his death on July 5, 2002, at age 83. His lifetime batting average of .344

is seventh all-time, and he won six batting titles. Williams' 521 career home runs and 1,839 runs batted in are 14th and 12th respectively.

He amassed those numbers even though he missed almost five seasons serving as a Marine pilot. He was stationed stateside in World War II, and he flew 39 combat missions during the Korean War.

"He was the best hitter I ever pitched to," Hall of Fame pitcher Bob Feller told the *Los Angeles Times*. "If it hadn't been for World War II and Korea, no one would have more records than Ted Williams."

"(Williams) was the best pure hitter I ever saw," Hall of Fame outfielder Joe DiMaggio said in 1991.

He was inducted into the National Baseball Hall of Fame in 1966, and named to Major League Baseball's All-Century Team in 1999. In his Hall of Fame induction speech in 1966, Williams talked about what got him there.

"(Ballplayers are) not born great hitters or pitchers or managers, and luck isn't a big factor. No one has come up with a substitute for hard work," he said.

For that reason, Williams disdained being called a "natural hitter." He said "nobody ever worked harder at hitting" than he did. His intense desire to excel pushed him to turn hitting a baseball into a science. He emphasized such things as proper weight distribution and hand positioning to get the most power out of his swing.

"The average hitter tries to hit the ball too hard. The secret of hitting is to get your power 100% from your forearms, wrists and hands," Williams said in "Hitter: The Life and Turmoil of Ted Williams" by Ed Linn.

Williams was the first power hitter to use a lighter bat; his ranged from 32 to 33 ounces. He rarely struck out, and said the lighter bat allowed him to wait longer on a pitch and thus be fooled less often. He maximized his natural instincts on hitting through his work ethic.

"Geniuses know. Einstein knew. Mozart knew. Ted Williams knew," Linn wrote.

Williams studied opposing pitchers the way he studied his swing in the mirror. He'd watch them carefully as they warmed up and during games to see if they were tipping off their pitches. He constantly examined what pitch patterns they fell into. Williams believed that people were likely to repeat their patterns.

"You can't outsmart the pitch," Williams believed, "but you can outsmart the pitcher."

"It was the mental dedication that marked him, though. The obsession with finding out everything he could about every pitcher he was going to face," Linn wrote.

Williams even checked out the weather. The first thing he did at a ballpark was to see which way the wind was blowing. Williams would then adjust by looking for base hits or home runs. "(Williams) always said to me, 'A little bit of wind affects a 100,000-pound aircraft. What do you think it does to a baseball?'" said former teammate Johnny Pesky.

Williams visualized success. He'd imagine what a pitcher was going to throw him and how he'd handle it. "The same way I was doing it in the backyard when I was a kid," he said. "Absolutely. I did that all my life."

He was selective at the plate and followed the simple advice given to him by the legendary Rogers Hornsby in 1938: Get a good ball to hit. Williams drew 2,019 walks in his career, fourth all-time; his .482 on-base percentage ranks first all-time. Williams' ability to identify close balls from strikes gave rise to a myth that his eyesight was superhuman.

Not so, he said. "A lot of people have 20-10 vision. The reason I saw things was that I was so intense. . . . I trained myself from a sandlotter to know that strike zone so I wouldn't be swinging at bad pitches. It was discipline, not super eyesight."

It was his physical discipline that let him become the oldest man to win a batting title, at age 40 in 1958; his average was .328. He'd also won it the previous year with a .388 average. To keep in shape, Williams "walked a lot, ran a little and did light weight work on the specific muscles he felt were most important when hitting," Linn wrote. Williams didn't smoke or drink, and he made sure he ate and went to sleep early. "The secret of Ted's baseball longevity was quite probably that he was never out of shape," Linn wrote.

Away from the ballpark, Williams focused on others. He served as longtime chairman of the fund-raising committee for the Jimmy Fund. The Jimmy Fund Hospital for Children's Cancer in Boston is one of the foremost cancer research centers in the world. Williams raised millions of dollars for the children.

When things didn't go his way during a game, the intense competitor in Williams didn't take it lightly. "A bad day should bother a ballplayer. I still can't sleep when I'm not hitting," he said.

The legacy Williams left baseball is one of perfection: "I have to admit that in my heart I always wanted to be the best, the best at the playground, the best in high school, the best on the team, the best in the league, no matter what it was. I think anybody competitive should feel that way."

8

Football Coach
Vince Lombardi

His Thirst For Perfection
Made His Players Champions

For Vince Lombardi, seeing the big picture was important. But it was the small things that won football games.

The Green Bay Packers coach's attention to detail was displayed in his favorite play. The Packers' signature was the power sweep, an end run that everyone knew was coming but, when properly executed, couldn't be stopped.

"They could go out to the practice field and drill the same play over and over until it was more than routine and familiar, it was in their blood, part of their reflexive being," David Maraniss wrote in "When Pride Still Mattered: A Life of Vince Lombardi."

That constant drilling turned Lombardi's Packers into a machine that won five league titles in the nine seasons he coached them, 1959–67. Lombardi's winning percentage is the best of any National Football League coach with at least 85 victories.

To make sure his players were as attentive to detail as he was, Lombardi (1913–70) drove them to focus on what they were doing each time they did it in practice.

"When a player made a mistake in practice, it was probably worse than in a game, because he was right there," said Hall of Fame defensive end Willie Davis, a 10-year Packer. "It made our practices much more focused and intense. By the time the game started, the mental part was second nature."

That approach carried over to Lombardi's personal life, too.

Lombardi was such a man of routine that Jim Huxford, who handled the sideline markers during Packer home games, knew he could wave as Lombardi entered the Catholic church at 7:56 a.m. each day if Huxford passed by, Maraniss wrote. Devoutly Catholic, Lombardi's religious background helped balance his career.

"In order to be the best coach, to keep winning, to stand out from his peers, he understood that at some level he had to . . . use some of his darker characteristics, especially his volatility, to his advantage," Maraniss said. "His temper and impatience, he once said, were characteristics that he was 'never able to subdue wholly.'"

Lombardi believed he wouldn't have been as effective a coach had he kept his emotions under tight control. His players agreed. "He was tough and demanding," said Hall of Fame quarterback Bart Starr. "But he was also a compassionate and very emotional person who could cry easily. And he had a marvelous sense of humor. That's a great blend."

Detailed Approach

Lombardi made sure to select assistant coaches who were as careful as he was. He asked them in job interviews about the most specific details of plays, down to how players made cuts as they ran. Packers assistant coach Red Cochran said he felt as if he'd been through an entrance exam to football graduate school after finishing the interview, Maraniss wrote.

Even in the office, Lombardi focused on every detail. He included all punctuation when he spoke into the Dictaphone, Maraniss noted. Typed letters went back to him for a final check of spelling.

Simply succeeding wasn't good enough for Lombardi. He wanted to make sure his players achieved success by doing the right things. Watching films the day after a game was tougher on players than games or practices.

"In films, even if you made a block, if you didn't do it correctly, you got a bigger ear-chewing," said Gale Gillingham, a three-time

All-Pro offensive guard. "Some films, after games, were holy terror hell. The attention was absolutely unmerciful."

Lombardi wouldn't accept failure and insisted his players strive to be the best.

"He said, 'We're going to relentlessly chase perfection,'" Starr recalled. "'We won't catch it, but if we constantly chase it, we'll achieve excellence.' Here was a person standing in front of you every day who wanted to be the very best. He wasn't interested in just being good. That's a great role model."

Lombardi understood the importance of being consistent.

"You can ramp people up for a one-time pursuit," Davis said. "But Lombardi used to say that continuing to win is an all-the-time, everyday process. You create the discipline and the commitment to make that happen. My willingness to do that today came from athletics."

Lombardi's disdain for losing was legendary. But he was able to learn from it.

He expected his players to do so, too. After the Packers lost 17–13 to the Philadelphia Eagles in the 1960 NFL championship game, Lombardi told his players, "Perhaps you didn't realize that you could have won this game. But I think there's no doubt in your minds now. And that's why you will win it all next year. This will never happen again. You will never lose another championship."

The Packers won the championship the next season, and never lost another playoff game he coached.

Take It To The Limit

Lombardi was able to drive his players to the brink of their limits. But at times, he went beyond. One of his unsung skills was to know when he'd pushed too far and his players needed a lift.

Jerry Kramer, a Packer offensive guard and five-time All Pro, recalls a time early in his career that Lombardi pushed him too far. The Packers had been sweating through a 90-degree workout in summer training camp. Kramer had made a few mistakes, including jumping offside on one play.

"He said to me, 'A college student's concentration level is five minutes, a high school student's is three minutes and for a kindergartner it's 30 seconds. You don't even have that, mister, so where the hell does that put you?'"

After the practice, Kramer was sitting in the locker room, pondering whether he even had a place in football. As Lombardi walked by, he told Kramer, "Son, one of these days you're going to be the best guard in football."

"That moment got my motor started," Kramer said. "That became my goal, and I pushed myself to accomplish that. That changed my whole attitude."

The Packers needed Lombardi's imposing presence to succeed, his players say.

"When you trace success through athletics or the corporate world, you find there's a strong personality and strong behavior behind it," said Davis, whose Los Angeles-based All Pro Broadcasting Inc. owns five radio stations. "There's an old saying: 'The speed of the leader is the speed of the organization.' The real timid and the easily subdued won't succeed."

Lombardi was neither, and he wasn't going to let anyone get in his way, including his bosses. He told the Packers' board of directors when he was hired that he wanted complete control. To show it, he took over team president Dominic Olejniczak's parking space, Maraniss wrote.

Lombardi's style came under criticism because he was so demanding and often demeaning. But his former players wouldn't have had it any other way.

"It's interesting what drives success," Davis said. "It's not always goody two-shoes. It's the discipline and overall culture you have to build. Sometimes it pushes the edge of being aggressive."

Lombardi's methods worked in the 1960s. Many wonder whether he would succeed today. His players have no doubts.

"No question about it," Starr said. "Look at what (former Miami Dolphin coach Don) Shula did. (Lombardi) was one of the most disciplined coaches around. The kind of people you want around you need that discipline. He'd have the same impact today."

9

Athlete
Babe Didrikson Zaharias
How She Became The Greatest
Sportswoman Of Her Time

O ther girls played with dolls. Babe Didrikson lifted weights. From the time she was a girl, she had boundless energy. But more than that, she had the drive to train hard not just in one field but also in all the major sports, from football to golf.

In fact, Babe Didrikson Zaharias (1911–56), who became the greatest female athlete of her generation, practiced golf swings not till her hands hurt but till they bled.

She played tennis hard too: "There was hardly a day I didn't wear holes in my socks. . . . I ran the soles off one pair of tennis shoes after another," she once said.

The Associated Press named Zaharias female athlete of the year six times. She won 10 major golf championships. She made the 1932 Olympic team and brought home two golds and one silver medal. She would have competed for more, but at the time women were restricted to just three Olympic events.

Some of her ability was inborn. Her mother, Hannah, was a famed skier and ice skater in Norway. But if Zaharias had natural talent, she had few resources to develop it. The native of Beaumont, Texas started out with materials you'd find in a junkyard.

Improvised Workouts

She worked out with barbells her father made from broomsticks and flat irons. Her family was too poor to give her 5 cents for a Saturday matinee, let alone buy her training gear.

So Zaharias learned to compensate in several ways.

She improvised. She used neighbors' hedges as hurdles. When one tall bush got in the way, she talked the neighbor into trimming it.

She turned her family's poverty to her advantage. To win, she used her need to prove that she was more than just a poor kid.

She bragged, getting an edge by psyching out her rivals. At 18, when Zaharias got to the track and field tryouts for the 1932 Olympics, she strutted around the infield hollering, "I'm going to win everything I enter!"

She came close. During the three-hour tryouts, she won six gold medals and broke four world records in eight events.

Her constant achievements built enormous self-confidence.

"She believed she could do anything — and she could," wrote Susan Cayleff in "Babe: The Life and Legend of Babe Didrikson Zaharias."

The biggest key to her success was her dedication to intense training.

"She often ran well into the dark hours and pushed herself beyond physical comfort," Cayleff wrote. "She was that way in every sport she took up."

One of her first coaches, Melvin McCombs, said, "Her only fault, as I have found it, is that she unconsciously and unknowingly overtrains."

When Zaharias was learning to golf, she often practiced 10 hours a day, hitting up to 1,500 balls. Her sister, Lillie, begged her to stop, but Zaharias said, "No, I (have) got to hit just a few more." On weekends, she practiced up to 16 hours a day.

Fierce Determination

When she picked up tennis, she played as many as 17 sets a day. Within a few months, she was beating her coach. "Once she was determined to fight, there seemed to be no stopping her," Cayleff wrote.

That grit served her best in 1952, when she was diagnosed with colon cancer. Although she was crushed at first, she soon met the disease head on.

"All my life I've been competing — and competing to win," she said. "I made up my mind that I was going to lick it all the way. . . . I was determined to come back and win golf championships just the same as before."

While her postoperative prognosis wasn't good, she wouldn't give up. Zaharias began exercising a few days after her operation by tightening her leg and arm muscles. A newspaper reported that during her recuperation she often took golf swings.

Four months after surgery, she was back on the golf course competing in a tournament.

Zaharias was so focused that she didn't let the mundane distract her. Unfortunately for her, that often included rules.

"She almost deliberately ignored them," Cayleff wrote. "Babe only excelled at things she chose to focus on, such as technique."

She was a racehorse with blinders. Often, her detachment from the technicalities of her sports came back to haunt her.

Zaharias was once barred from a major tennis tournament. Only amateurs were allowed to compete. She was a professional and hadn't bothered to check the rules.

For all her bravado, Zaharias was a worrier.

The night before her Olympic trials, she couldn't sleep because of severe stomach pain, likely brought on by anxiety. But she learned to use it to her advantage, too. She read pain "as a signal that she was 'really ready' to compete," Cayleff wrote.

10

Coach George Haines
Innovative And Caring
Approach Helped Him Push
Swimmers To The Top

For George Haines, developing championship swimmers in the pool started by setting an example for them out of it.

"I set my standards high for me and for the kids that swam for me. I expected a lot out of them. I think I led a decent, wholesome quality of life, and I think my athletes responded to that," Haines said in an interview.

A seven-time Olympics swimming coach, Haines was inducted into the International Swimming Hall of Fame in 1974. In 2001 he was voted the swimming coach of the century by that organization and by *Swimming World* magazine. His swimmers won a total of 44 Olympic gold medals, along with 14 silver and 10 bronze medals.

"George sort of combined the gruff no-nonsense coach with the fatherly image, so that even if he was telling you to go back and do it again or do it better, there was a tone in his voice or an expression on his face that let you know that he expected better out of you because he saw it inside of you. He inspired people to want to do their best for him," said Phillip Whitten, who swam for Haines and is currently *Swimming World*'s editor in chief.

Haines, a native of Huntington, Ind., modeled himself after his own swimming coach, Glen S. Hummer.

"I used to sit in the front seat of the car with (Hummer) coming home from swimming meets for two reasons. First, to keep him awake. And the second one was to ask him questions about swimming, because I knew at a young age (coaching) was what I wanted to do," Haines said.

"He always told me that a coach had to be as fair as possible, and never to show favoritism. Every coach has to make sure he's going to feel or be for the underdog kid as much as you are for those who've got a lot of talent."

Whether at his Santa Clara Swim Club in California, which he began in 1950, or as the head swimming coach at Santa Clara High School or the University of California, Los Angeles, Haines kept in mind that his swimmers were all different.

"George believed in tailoring programs to individuals. He was flexible, and he was open to new training techniques," said Donna de Varona, who won an Olympic gold medal in 1964. "When I came from one club to his, he wanted to know what I had done, and he incorporated my workout (routine) in his program."

"George wasn't one of those people who accepted whatever the conventional wisdom was at that particular moment," Whitten said. "He was always looking for the best way to get the most out of his athletes."

Many times Haines had several of his swimmers competing against each other at the same meets or at the Olympics. Yet he could still say to each of his swimmers before the race that he honestly believed he or she could win it.

"He could get you to focus on what your strengths were, and on what you had to do to be successful to win a race," said Chris von Saltza, who won an Olympic gold medal in 1960.

Haines worked to foster a team atmosphere in what's essentially an individual sport. He planned practices so that, whenever possible, all the swimmers finished at the same time. He didn't want some working hard in the pool while others were resting in the locker room.

"We talked about team all the time," Haines said. "When we went to a meet, and I did this as an Olympic coach too, I made every kid on the team aware of the first event. . . . That first event is the most important event in the meet. The team would be there to encourage those guys in the first event. And if they swam really well, then I could turn around to the others and say, 'See that? Man, those guys swam good. And if they can swim like that, look how ready you are.' And it worked."

Haines was among the first to introduce two daily practices. But he was careful not to burn out his swimmers.

"We worked hard, but our workload wasn't unbearable," said Claudia Colb, who won an Olympic gold medal in 1968.

Mark Spitz, who won seven gold medals and set seven world records at the 1972 Olympics, swam for Haines as a teen-ager.

"George Haines taught me how to become a champion," Spitz said. "I remember the first time I broke a world record. He said to me, 'Everybody will know what you did in the newspaper tomorrow. You've just gone from the hunter to the hunted, and you will now spend the rest of your life trying to stay on top.' And he was oh so right."

Haines didn't accept obstacles. Instead, he found ways around them. For example, in the absence of a 50-meter pool to practice in early in his career, he took his swimmers to a local reservoir and had them train there.

"George made practice fun and creative," de Varona said. "We never had two workouts the same. Many coaches these days just put the workout on the board, and it's the same day in and day out. Swimming is very tedious, so you really have to make it interesting."

Nearly 5% of the swimmers inducted into the International Swimming Hall of Fame trained under Haines, including de Varona, von Saltza, Colb and Spitz. They learned from him, and he's learned from them.

"I think if you had to name one thing that every champion has, it's they want it more than anybody else and they have great desire to be the best," Haines said.

11

Harold "Red" Grange

The Galloping Ghost Helped Rush Pro Football Toward Respectability

For a short halfback, facing Michigan's football powerhouse was certainly a challenge.

But Harold "Red" Grange loved nothing like a challenge. This one presented itself in 1924 before the opening game at the University of Illinois' new Memorial Stadium.

Michigan-Illinois was a clash of 2-0 teams that had gone unbeaten the year before. Yet it sounded as though the visiting Wolverines had the upper hand. Their ex-coach, Fielding Yost, figured they could handle the Illini, who were on a 10-game winning streak that had begun in 1922. Yost boasted that Michigan would stop the 5-foot-11, 175-pound Grange, the Illini's gridiron hero.

Such a challenge was like the wind to Grange, known as "The Galloping Ghost" for his fleet and sure-footed field performances. In front of 67,000 fans, he scored four touchdowns in the first 12 minutes — a feat that has yet to be repeated.

Nor did he stop with that thrust. After a brief rest, he strode back into the game for a fifth touchdown on the way to amassing 402 rushing yards. He also passed 20 yards for a sixth touchdown, noted Benjamin Rader in "American Sports." Illinois beat Michigan 39–14.

While his feats at that game inspired noted sportswriter Grantland Rice to give him his nickname, they weren't isolated. A charter member of the College and Pro Football Halls of Fame, the red-headed Grange (1903–91) remains one of the best football players ever.

A three-time All-American halfback, he scored 31 touchdowns and rushed for 3,637 yards in three seasons at Illinois, and became the most famous player of his time. His decisions to turn pro and help found the American Football League changed spectator sports forever.

Grange was "three or four men rolled into one for football purposes," wrote Damon Runyon. "He is Jack Dempsey, Babe Ruth, Al Jolson, Paavo Nurmi and Man O' War. Put together, they spell Grange."

Humble Beginnings

Born to a homemaker and a lumber foreman in Forksville, Pa., Grange was the last of five children. The family was happy until his mother died when Grange was 5. Devastated, his father, Lyle, moved his family to Wheaton, Ill., some 30 miles west of Chicago, to start anew.

He became the town's police chief, but didn't earn much. Lyle sent his three daughters back to Pennsylvania because he felt his wife's family members would better raise them. His boys remained with him.

Without much money in the family, Grange had just three outlets: school, chores and sports. Seeking to make the best of the situation, he flung himself into sports of every kind with friends. He played games daily, finding space in vacant lots and converted barn lofts.

His natural skill coupled with relentless practice paid off. Grange earned 16 letters in football, baseball, basketball and track while at Wheaton High School.

Knowing his ability could result in a college scholarship, Grange was determined to keep himself in top shape during both the playing season and the summer. In addition to practices and games, he sought the most physically demanding part-time job around to work his muscles: hauling ice.

Once at Illinois, Grange leaned toward joining the basketball and track teams. Fraternity brothers, however, saw his finesse with a football and worked to persuade him to stick to it. Knowing a good argument when he heard it, Grange heeded their advice.

Grange also knew when he needed help. A soft-spoken and reluctant hero, Grange saw that his skill and popularity could be profitable. So he turned to Champaign, Ill., storeowner Charles Pyle to help him out.

Pyle, who had many business acquaintances, knew that Chicago Bears owner/coach George Halas wanted a big attraction on his team to pump up the gate. He put Grange in touch with Halas. The day after playing his last game for Illinois, Grange signed a $100,000 contract to play for Halas' and co-owner Dutch Sternaman's Bears.

It was a move that outraged many. Pro football was known as "a dirty little business run by rogues and bargain-basement entrepreneurs," wrote John Carroll in "Red Grange and the Rise of Modern Football."

By leaving school, Grange sparked a national debate by openly flaunting "the myth of the college athlete as a gentleman-amateur who played merely for the fun of the game and the glory of his school," said Rader. Even Grange's Illinois coach, Robert Zuppke, condemned him.

The Barnstormer

But Grange ignored the critics and steamed forward. Barnstorming across the country for a grueling 17 exhibition games during the 1925–26 season, he worked as hard as ever on the field. Grange gave it his all, swiveling through defensive lines as if they weren't there.

He couldn't win on his own, though, and Grange was quick to give credit to others for helping him.

"I hope a little bit of my plaque will be owned by every teammate that I ever had the privilege of playing with," he said in his Football Hall of Fame induction speech in 1963. "I think it's wonderful to be involved with all these gentlemen here at my rear, fellas that I have played with, fellas that I have played against. I feel that I am extremely flattered to be in their company."

Grange might've been quiet, but he stood his ground when he thought he was right. When he, Halas and Pyle couldn't agree on a new contract in 1926, Pyle and Grange started the American Football League with Grange as the star attraction on the New York Giants.

After missing part of 1927 and all of 1928 with a knee injury, Grange returned to the Bears in 1929 and played with them until 1935.

When opportunity arrived — even while he was injured — Grange jumped for it. He capitalized on his enormous recognition, inking endorsement deals for Red Grange dolls, a sweater, gum, soda and even a meatloaf, according to "Champions of American Sport," edited by Marc Pachter. Grange and Pyle got a share of the gate at games, splitting $250,000 in their first year of partnership.

After retiring from football, Grange stayed devoted to the game. He served as a Bears coach for four years, later becoming a football announcer in the 1940s and 1950s.

His entire life, however, Grange stayed modest about his achievements. He preferred to put them in perspective. "They built my accomplishments way out of proportion," he said. "I never got the idea that I was a tremendous big shot. I could carry a football well, but there are a lot of doctors and teachers and engineers who could do their thing better than I."

PART 2

Clearing The Toughest Hurdles

© Hulton-Deutsch Collection/CORBIS

It takes concentration and dedication to excel in sports. There are always diversions, but if you want to excel in track and field, or anything else, you have to be willing to make some sacrifices. That's where discipline comes in.

— JESSE OWENS

12

Blind Climber
Erik Weihenmayer

He Faced Down Fear To Reach
The Top Of The World

People who are afraid to fail become frozen in time. They are forever afraid to take risks, forever afraid to dare, forever afraid to succeed. Erik Weihenmayer isn't one of those people.

Weihenmayer's life has been one of majestic triumphs over terrible fears.

When Erik was 6 months old, doctors discovered that he had retinoscheses, an eye disorder that would slowly destroy his retinas. He grew up knowing he didn't have long to see the world around him. By the age of 13, he was totally blind.

Many people would've immediately set limits on themselves, deciding that blindness would prevent them from being active.

Weihenmayer decided to see just how much he could do. Today, he's a world-class athlete, an acrobatic skydiver, long-distance biker, marathon runner, skier, scuba diver and member of the College Wrestling Hall of Fame.

He's also climbed the three highest mountains in the world. On May 23, 2001, he was on a team of 12 climbers who pushed to the top of Mount Everest. One of his fellow climbers, at 64, became the oldest person to reach the summit. Weihenmayer, then 32, made the 29,000-foot climb as the first blind person to conquer the legendary mountain.

"All my life," Weihenmayer once said, "fear of failure had nearly paralyzed me."

The important word is "nearly." Weihenmayer experienced more than his share of fear. But he didn't succumb to it. He used it.

Failure, for Weihenmayer, isn't a disgrace — it's a component of success. It provides an opportunity to learn the skills that lead to success.

"Most people don't take risks because they are afraid to fail, to embarrass themselves," said Ed Weihenmayer, Erik's father. "Erik has the courage to fail. That's why the near impossible has become routine for him."

A Teachable Moment

Weihenmayer treats fear with a healthy respect; he's not a daredevil full of bravado who stupidly ignores risk.

"He's one of the top mountaineers in the country," said Gavin Atwood, who trained for the Everest climb with Weihenmayer and trekked with him into the Everest base camp. "He got that way by confronting his fears and learning from them."

Before scaling Mount Everest, on a training climb up Mount Rainier, Weihenmayer had to set up a tent on a snowfield.

Weihenmayer laid the tent on the snow. He tried and tried to shove a pole into one of the tent sleeves. But his thick gloves made the job impossible.

Recounting the incident in his book, "Touch the Top of the World," Weihenmayer said he took his glove off so he could actually feel the pole.

"But sharp splinters of sleet pricked my skin bare, and it went instantly numb," he said. "I stuffed my lifeless hand back inside the glove and beat it against my knee. When it came back to life, the pain was so intense I almost vomited from nausea."

He'd failed. His teammates had to finish the job for him. The pain in his hand, Weihenmayer said, was nothing "compared with my frustration and embarrassment, like a balloon expanding in my chest."

Weihenmayer wanted to turn his fear of failure to his advantage. After returning home to Phoenix, he took the tent, poles and gloves to a field and started a rigorous practice session.

"The temperature was more than 100 degrees," his father said. "Erik put on the thick gloves, and over and over and over he practiced setting up the tent. He did not want to ever be the weak link on the team again."

Today, Weihenmayer can set up a tent faster than his sighted comrades.

Through persistence, Weihenmayer discovered that the small acts — taken together — lead to success.

"When Erik wanted to climb the nose of El Capitan in Yosemite Valley, a 3,300-foot rock wall, he spent a month learning how to haul equipment up a mountain, how to place pitons in cracks, how to sleep overnight on a ledge and dozens of other skills," Atwood said. "He's an important member of each team he climbs with. No one says, 'OK, you're blind. We'll haul your stuff and take care of you.' He does his job."

Weihenmayer has to innovate to make up for his blindness. He rakes his fingers across the rock face to feel for cracks that will give him a handhold or foothold as he climbs. He plunges his ax into the ice and listens to the sound it makes to discern hard ice from soft ice. By methodically testing the ice in front of him, he's climbed sheer ice walls unassisted.

He relies on others to do what he can't, listening for shouted directions from his teammates to gauge his next move. "We yell out, 'There's a great crack to your right, loose rocks on the left,' stuff like that," Atwood said.

Constructive Risks

There've been times when Weihenmayer's fears got the best of him, times when he couldn't redirect them in such a rational and constructive way.

"When he knew his sight was going, when total blindness was coming, he rebelled against living in the blind world," his father said. "He would go with his friends and jump off a 40-foot cliff into a shallow stream. There was one, small deep part. If you missed that spot, you could be killed. He was trying to prove that he could still see."

Erik credits his parents' love and common sense with getting him through this period. Both parents felt there was nothing to be gained from preventing him from taking reasonable risks.

"A meaningful life is all about taking constructive risks, whether you succeed or not," his father said.

They both encouraged Erik to reach higher and higher, to never feel limited by his handicap, and both were there to catch him when he reached too high. Particularly close to his mother, Erik turned to her to help guide him through all of his early ordeals.

Then further tragedy struck. The same year Weihenmayer went totally blind, his mother died in a car crash.

The young man who'd conquered his fear of physical failure was forced to deal with and overcome devastating emotional fears.

Of the day when his father told him about the accident, Erik wrote, "How can I explain the pain that surged through me? If I had gone blind a thousand times, the pain would have been nothing by comparison. If I could have died that day by only choosing it, I would have died instantly. How could it be, the person who had savagely protected me all my life was gone?"

Slowly, instead of retreating into self-pity, Erik began facing the pain inside. He actively looked for ways to ease the sadness. When he was alone in the family home, for example, he'd lie down and call up good memories of their time together.

"Other times, I'd sit in her closet surrounded by all her coats and dresses, trying to lose myself in the familiar fragrance, trying to pretend that if her smell was there, she must be there, too," he wrote.

Now, Weihenmayer uses his mother's memory and his father's continuing devotion as sources of strength. "I see them," he wrote, "as a broom and a dustpan. My father was the broom, sweeping me out into the world. When I shattered, my mom would pick up the pieces."

Weihenmayer is modest about his achievements. Rather than focusing too much on what he's done, he looks for new ways to challenge himself to get to the next level.

"It's always, 'What's next?'" his father said.

13

Speed Skater Eric Heiden
Fierce Dedication Helped Him
Become An Olympic Champion

Eric Heiden was dead tired. He'd stayed up into the wee hours watching the dramatic U.S. victory over the Soviet Union in the hockey showdown the night before in the 1980 Winter Olympics. Now, on the morning of the biggest race of his life, the world's best speed skater could barely open his eyes.

In a few hours, the 21-year-old Heiden was to compete in the 10,000-meter speed-skating final at Lake Placid, N.Y. He'd already won the 500-, 1,000-, 1,500- and 5,000-meter events. If he captured the 10,000 meters, he'd snare an unprecedented fifth gold medal, a feat thought impossible by peers and observers.

His coach, Dianne Holum, dragged him out of bed to the cafeteria, where he wolfed down handfuls of bread for a quick carbohydrate boost. Hours later, Heiden won the gold in record time, capping a performance that ranks with the best in Olympic history.

How'd he do it?

For starters, he built on his natural ability. Gifted with an athletic physique, he focused on keeping himself in top condition, even as a youth. When he was just 10 years old, coaches and older skaters noted his remarkable poise and confidence.

"He was the most talented, gifted and dedicated boy I ever met," said his former trainer, Gunter Traub, on the "50 Greatest Athletes" special on cable TV channel ESPN in 1999.

Eager To Excel

Inspired by their grandfather, who was a former hockey player, and by their supportive parents, Heiden and his younger sister, Beth, spent countless hours playing and training for a variety of sports.

The Heidens wanted their children to excel at whatever they were interested in, so they turned the living room of their Madison, Wis., home into a full-scale gymnasium, complete with pommel horse and rings.

To stay in peak form, Heiden and his sister constantly competed with each other. They ran, skated and did pull-ups to the point of exhaustion. Both would eventually compete in the Olympics.

Eric Heiden's workouts were so tough that other athletes were aghast. "Eric was a freak of nature," said Dan Jansen, a speed-skating gold medalist in the 1994 Winter Olympics. Heiden's contemporaries said they could handle only about 30% of his typical grueling workout.

Those close to him say Heiden's mental strength exceeds even his physical prowess. "He was able to look inside himself and dig deep for the strength that he had," said Leah Poulus Mueller, an Olympic teammate. "Sometimes the pressure made him skate even better. He wasn't afraid of it. It was a challenge to him."

Heiden knew he was good. But he shied away from the limelight, keeping a low profile and eschewing interviews and tributes. He knew that if he developed a swelled head, he might lose sight of his goals.

In fact, Heiden insisted he live life on his terms. His terms meant keeping the media and intense fans at arm's length. He was always polite and cordial with his followers, but he tried to conduct his everyday affairs as normally as possible.

Heiden competed in the 1976 Winter Olympics in Innsbruck, Austria, at age 17, but didn't win a medal. He first captured public attention a year later, when he won the world championships in the Netherlands, a country mad for speed skating. After that performance, Heiden became a household name in the Netherlands and in Norway.

Mike Woods, later a teammate of Heiden's, recalled that on travels to places where locals treated speed-skating champions with reverence, "People were grabbing his clothes — it was sometimes hard to be with him."

Heiden's five golds in 1980 rank with Mark Spitz's seven golds in the 1972 Summer Games as two of the best Olympic performances of all time. During and soon after the 1980 Games, Heiden began to receive the same hero's treatment he'd garnered years before in Europe.

Time magazine brought Heiden in two nights before his fifth event for a photo shoot. *Time*'s editors wanted him to pose with five gold medals around his neck, since the magazine's presses would begin running before the skater could compete for his fifth gold. Heiden was reticent. He didn't want to appear overconfident.

Yet he believed in himself. Finally, he agreed, but he insisted on owning the rights to the photographs "so that he wouldn't be exploited as time went on," said *Time*'s Judith Stoller.

It was a wise decision. When the Games ended, endorsement offers flooded in. Sneaker companies, cereal makers and soft drink vendors all wanted Heiden's smiling face adorning their products. Young, good-looking, immensely popular and successful, Heiden could've been swept up in the praise and adulation.

Instead, he stuck to his guns. He kept the photos out of commercial circulation. He decided he'd lend his name only to products he believed in. He worked with Crest, for instance, because he used the toothpaste in his everyday life.

New Day, New Challenge

Heiden found himself surrounded by the public. But he didn't want to be known as someone who'd won some Olympic medals and then never did anything else.

Heiden quickly found a new purpose: cycling. He saw that the sport required skills similar to speed skating. And it had an added benefit: It was another challenge to meet.

"It was something I wanted to try," Heiden said. "Like with skating, I wanted to see what my limits were."

Limits? Heiden applied the same workout techniques he'd used in speed skating to cycling. He spent hours in grueling workouts. He timed himself carefully when he got on his bike. He watched his diet. He studied previous cycling champs for insights into their style.

After showing steady improvement for a few years, he won the U.S. Pro Cycling title in 1985.

In 1986, he competed in the prestigious Tour de France for the first time. In the French Alps, Heiden fell off his bike, banging his head on the ground. The nasty crash abruptly ended his cycling career.

Never one to sit still for long, Heiden decided it was time for a new challenge — this time, a mental one. He enrolled in medical school at Stanford University that fall, with an eye toward following in his father's footsteps as an orthopedic surgeon.

"So many athletes live on (their success) for the rest of their lives and really are half-people," said *Washington Post* reporter Sally Jenkins, who's covered Heiden extensively. "Not him. He's a whole human being."

He approached medical school the same way he approached athletics — with total focus on his goal. He mapped out a strict study schedule. He looked for help before he needed it to make sure he understood everything he was reading. He worked to stay in good physical shape to ensure his solid mental conditioning.

Today, Heiden, 44, practices as an orthopedic surgeon and is on the faculty at the University of California, Davis, Medical School. His doctor's acumen and athletic background have made him a hit with patients, especially athletes. Former patients include Ruthie Bolton-Holifield, a Women's National Basketball Association player who quickly recovered from a torn anterior cruciate ligament in her knee thanks to Heiden's help.

Said Olympic teammate Tom Plant: "He shows you what can be achieved if you set goals and focus on your goals."

14

Jim Thorpe Earned
The Gold
Visualization Pushed Him To
Peak Performance

The decision by the Amateur Athletic Union was final. Jim Thorpe would be stripped of his two gold medals from the 1912 Olympics in Sweden, his name removed from athletic annals and his records expunged.

Thorpe was guilty of playing semiprofessional baseball for two seasons, which voided his amateur status and Olympic medals.

Thorpe was forthright and humble about his mistake. "I hope I will be partly excused by the fact that I was simply an Indian schoolboy and did not know that I was doing wrong. I was not very wise in the ways of the world," he told the athletic union.

Other athletes had played semipro sports in the off-season, but they used fake names. Thorpe used his real name.

James Francis Thorpe, the greatest athlete in the world, was stripped of his proudest achievement: receiving the gold medal — and setting a world record that stood for 15 years — in the Olympic decathlon. The decathlon is a series of 10 events and is the ultimate test of strength, endurance, stamina and spring. Thorpe also won gold in the pentathlon, becoming the first and only athlete to win both events in the same Olympics. The second-place winners of those two events refused to accept what was Thorpe's gold.

If Thorpe was angered by the decision, he didn't let it show. Not until years later did he comment on it. He took comfort in that millions of Americans thought he was still the greatest of all amateur athletes. After the Olympic decision, he chose to just move on. More than anything else, he was first, last and always a competitor. He knew other opportunities would come.

A few months later, Thorpe negotiated one of the largest baseball contracts of that time: a three-year, $5,000 deal to play for the New York Giants, and later with the Boston Braves. He played in the 1913 World Series.

Halls Of Fame

He was also a highly gifted football player, becoming a member of the college and pro football halls of fame. He's also in the U.S. Track & Field Hall of Fame and the U.S. Olympic Hall of Fame.

Thorpe is considered by many to be the only American athlete to excel in three major sports: track and field, football and baseball. He played pro football and baseball concurrently for seven years.

In a poll of Associated Press sportswriters in 1950, Thorpe was voted the half-century's Greatest All-Around Male Athlete, with a score well ahead of the No. 2 choice, Babe Ruth. Thorpe was also chosen as the greatest football player of the half-century.

He was skillful in a host of other sports, including tennis, golf, gymnastics, rowing, lacrosse, bowling and billiards — even ballroom dancing.

Thorpe, part Indian and part Irish, was born in 1887 on an Indian reservation in Prague, Okla. His twin brother died when he was 9. Both his parents died when he was a teen-ager.

Thorpe's athletic potential was evident at an early age. When he was 10, Thorpe ran home from school, cross country, for 18 miles. This was after he'd walked 23 miles earlier that day.

It was at the Carlisle Indian School in Pennsylvania that his athleticism was noticed.

One afternoon at Carlisle, Thorpe watched the track team practice the high jump. When the bar was set at 5 feet, 9 inches, which no one there could jump, Thorpe stepped up and asked to try. He was in overalls and tennis shoes, having never high-jumped before. He cleared the bar with ease and grace.

It was classic Thorpe: always looking for a challenge.

"I never was content unless I was trying my skill in some game against my fellow playmates or testing my endurance and wits against some member of the animal kingdom," he once said.

An assistant football coach introduced Thorpe to Pop Warner, one of the greatest track and football coaches of all time. Later, Warner called Thorpe the greatest all-around athlete.

Did It All

In football, Thorpe could do it all. For each game, he played halfback, defensive back, punter and place-kicker. He once punted the football 88 yards. He kicked a 48-yard field goal that helped Carlisle beat Harvard University. That year, in 1912, Carlisle won the Collegiate Football Championship, beating powerhouse teams from Syracuse, Pittsburgh, Nebraska, Penn State and Army. Thorpe was named All-American, having scored 25 touchdowns and 198 points in the season.

When he played professional football, Thorpe's Canton Bulldogs won championships in 1916, 1917 and 1919. He is considered to be the first football superstar before the age of television. In 1920, he was the first president of an organization now called the National Football League. The NFL's Most Valuable Player award is known as the Jim Thorpe Trophy.

He frequently angered coaches by his seemingly lackadaisical attitude toward practice. But that wasn't the case; Thorpe said he practiced by sitting and visualizing what he wanted to achieve.

Thorpe was so confident in his running ability as a halfback that in one game he told opposing players several times where he'd run on the next play, daring them to tackle him. They couldn't.

He retired from football in 1928 at age 41.

By the time the 1930s Depression arrived, Thorpe was nearly broke. Beset with marital problems and his sports career over, Thorpe drifted to Hollywood in search of fame and glory. He did get some bit parts, but not enough to make a living for himself, his wife and four children.

He didn't let that get him down. He took jobs as a painter, ditch digger, guard and bouncer — whatever could help him pay the bills. He didn't brag about his illustrious sports career, but he did continue to train on his own. It made him feel good, he said.

In 1932, when reports surfaced that Thorpe was nearly broke and unable to attend the Olympic Games in Los Angeles, help poured in from all over. He sat at the L.A. Coliseum with the vice president of the United States.

His name returned to the sports pages in 1950 when Thorpe was selected as the outstanding male athlete and greatest football player of the half-century. A movie of his life was rushed into production.

Thorpe died in 1953 of a heart attack, his third, at age 64. He was living in a trailer in Lomita, Calif.

But his inspiration lived on. In 1983, after decades of appeals by members of Congress and his family, the International Olympic Committee restored Thorpe's records and presented replicas of his medals to his family.

Thorpe, who was nearly forgotten after he left sports, has more recently been honored in numerous ways. In 1999, for example, the Senate and House passed a resolution that named Thorpe "America's Athlete of the 20th Century."

15

Soccer Great Ronaldo
He Kicked Up His Tenacity To
Realize World Cup Goals

It's obvious that Brazil's Ronaldo knows how to win soccer games. But his real talent lies in setting his own goals and hammering away until he reaches the back of the net.

The Brazilian striker's career fell into jeopardy in the spring of 2000. Three times before, Ronaldo had injured ligaments in his right knee. He did rehab and came back. But six minutes into the Italian Cup final, pitting Inter Milan against Lazio, Ronaldo got chopped from behind. The healed ligament snapped. The Inter Milan star collapsed to the pitch, writhing in pain.

Few athletes suffer such serious injuries and bounce back to their original form. Ronaldo vowed to be one who did. So when he arrived back home in Brazil after another round of surgery in Europe, he pursued an intensive schedule of recovery.

"I was in Rio one day to interview Ronaldo, and it is amazing the amount of effort he puts in to reach an objective," said Alexandre Barros, Portuguese site editor of SoccerAge.com. "When I interviewed him, he practiced and did physiotherapy sessions for eight hours in one day. This is the kind of commitment this guy has. He doesn't lose focus."

From Nov. 21, 1999, to Sept. 20, 2001, "Phenomeno" played just seven minutes of competitive soccer. But he refused to give up on his dream of joining the ranks of fellow Brazilian Pelé and others who won the World Cup for Brazil.

At the 2002 World Cup, co-hosted by Japan and South Korea, Ronaldo showed no signs of the bum right knee. With a 2–0 win over three-time Cup holder Germany, Ronaldo — whose full name is Ronaldo Luiz Nazario de Lima — and the Brazilian side claimed a record fifth gold trophy.

In the final, Brazil's top forward with the No. 9 jersey slotted in the match's two goals to bring his scoring total in World Cup play to 12 goals, tying the world's most famous player of all time, Pelé.

"We had a lot of difficulties coming into this tournament, but we have won it because of an amazing mentality," said Brazil coach Luiz Felipe Scolari. "It is one the players, with Ronaldo so prominent, displayed so strongly throughout this World Cup. It is the mentality which just does not accept being second."

Determined To Play

Born in 1976 in a modest suburb of Rio de Janeiro, Ronaldo knew at an early age he wanted to become a professional soccer player. He played street soccer, and then an indoor version called futebol de salao. But success came slowly. Ronaldo's favorite club, Flamengo, the famous Rio club that helped breed Zico and other top players, rejected him at a tryout because it didn't want to pay the bus fares to and from his windowless, doorless home in Bento Ribeiro. On the bus ride home, a gang mugged him, taking his newly bought watch.

Ronaldo didn't take the rejection in stride. Still determined to play soccer for a living, he quit high school at age 13 to join Sao Cristovao, a minor pro team in the suburbs of Rio. His scoring prowess attracted more and more scouts. At the age of 16, Ronaldo's contract was sold to a bigger Brazilian club named Cruzeiro.

At the 1994 World Cup in the U.S., Ronaldo earned his first championship while sitting on the bench the whole time. His mother asked on public TV, "Why do you never let that Ronaldinho play?" referring to Ronaldo, according to R9ronaldo.com, a fan club Web site. (At the 1994 Cup, his name was Ronaldinho.) But Ronaldo himself never complained publicly. He watched and learned as much as he could from team leaders Romario and Juninho.

After the 1994 Cup, Ronaldo further developed his game by competing in the top European leagues: first at PSV Eindhoven in the

Netherlands, then Barcelona, Spain, and finally Internazionale in Milan, Italy. These experiences helped Ronaldo gain knowledge about the styles of other countries' play, serving him and his teammates well in the World Cup.

When the World Cup made its France stop in 1998, Ronaldo seemed to shoulder all of his country's dreams. The pressure was so great that hours before the final between host France and Brazil, Ronaldo apparently suffered convulsions. Doctors found nothing wrong, and Ronaldo played. But France beat the champions 3–0. Ronaldo played like a zombie, soccer writers said.

After that loss, Ronaldo suffered his repeated knee injuries. Brazil barely qualified for the 2002 World Cup. Still, the then-25-year-old "Extraterrestre" (Portuguese for alien) believed in himself and shut down his fears.

"A Brazilian footballer always knows there will be shadows from time to time," Ronaldo told the *Independent* of London on the eve of Brazil's win over England in the World Cup quarterfinals. "It is impossible not to expect them when you know that so much importance is attached to what you do. But . . . there is always the dream. It is that you will conquer your fears, and when it matters most you will find power you never had before."

Passion, Practicality And Teamwork

Soccer journalists praise Ronaldo for his sturdy, 6-foot frame and explosive speed. Others say his technique falls short of Pelé and other Brazilian greats. But perhaps no player can match his great passion and tenacity, fueled by his love for scoring goals.

In the 2002 World Cup final against Germany, Ronaldo fell to the ground after losing the ball to a German defender. He quickly got up, snatched the ball back and flicked it to fellow forward Rivaldo. Ronaldo raced toward the goal, perhaps expecting a through ball.

Rivaldo didn't comply. He sent a well-struck shot that bounced off the chest of German keeper Oliver Kahn, who had given up just one goal in the tourney. This time Kahn failed to bury the shot into his chest, and the ball was loose for fractions of a second. Racing between two flat-footed German players, Ronaldo stuck in the game's first goal in the 67th minute.

"When the goalkeeper saw into whose path he had directed it, his blood ran cold. Ronaldo swooped, and the match, you knew in your bones, was over," James Lawton wrote in the *Independent*. Ronaldo hammered the last nail into the coffin 12 minutes later.

Ronaldo adopts a businesslike approach to his schedule each day.

"He is a very responsible player. He is a guy who never misses a day of training, who is never late," Barros of SoccerAge.com said.

After leaving his native Brazil to play for Dutch powerhouse PSV Eindhoven, Ronaldo sought advice from experts regarding every part of his game and career. Early on, he hired a team of doctors, physiotherapists and marketing experts to help him succeed.

Ronaldo knows his success depends a lot on his teammates, and lets it be known. After the Brazil squad returned to the locker room following its World Cup victory over Germany at Yokohama International Stadium in Japan, Ronaldo hugged every teammate and thanked him, midfielder Roberto Carlos said in a TV interview.

16

Track Champion Jesse Owens

His Desire And Discipline Made Him A Legend

Young James Cleveland "Jesse" Owens lost his first race. But the way he figured it later, he still came out a winner.

Owens (1913–80) was in the eighth grade and running a quarter-mile race. He was leading after 100 yards, but then heard footsteps: Two older boys were catching up fast.

Owens looked to his right and saw the boys pulling even with him. He then clenched his teeth, tensed his body and narrowed his eyes. The two boys passed Owens, who wound up finishing fourth.

Owens was crushed. He said dejectedly to his coach, Charles Riley, "I thought I'd win. . . . Why didn't I?"

"Because you tried to stare them down instead of run them down," Riley said.

Instead of channeling his energy into his running, Owens was placing great effort into appearing outwardly determined, Riley told him.

Owens never forgot the lesson. "The determination, every last bit of it that I could get up, had to be on the inside," Owens wrote with Paul Neimark in "Jesse: The Man Who Outran Hitler."

Riley further taught Owens that if he concentrated on getting his form just right, he'd run faster. In time, Owens developed a fluid style that made him appear to be running without exertion.

Being the best was important to Owens.

"God has given everyone the ability to do something," Owens wrote in "Track and Field." "Once you discover where your ability is, you must concentrate on developing it."

Owens went on to dominate the 1936 Olympic Games in Berlin and become a legend. He won four gold medals and destroyed German dictator Adolf Hitler's propaganda myth of Aryan athletic superiority.

In 1950, The Associated Press named Owens the greatest track-and-field athlete in history.

Dreams Can Become Reality

He was born into poverty in Oakville, Ala. Owens' father, the son of a former slave, was an ill-educated, struggling sharecropper. The seventh of eight children, Jesse was a sickly child who almost died.

But he was also a dreamer. When the son of his father's employer told young Jesse he was planning to go to college one day, Jesse immediately announced to his family that he'd one day go also. The dream inspired him to study hard, and he aimed to be the best in his class at school.

Eventually, Owens attended Ohio State University. He wrote four books in the 1970s, two of which dealt with social issues for black Americans. "In America, anyone can still become somebody," Owens said.

Marlene Rankin, Owens' daughter, said, "My father believed in being persistent, taking initiative and being focused." Rankin is executive director of the Jesse Owens Foundation in Chicago, which helps youths realize their academic, athletic and social potential.

Jesse's mother moved the family north to Cleveland when he was a child to escape Southern racism. She hoped Cleveland would mean a better life for her family. It did for young Jesse.

"How does the sickly son of a humbler-than-humble Southern Negro sharecropper come from death's door to be 'the world's fastest human'?" Owens wrote in "The Jesse Owens Story." "The answer lies in different things. Wanting to be something so bad you can hardly sit still is part of it. Hating poverty is another. But maybe the most important thing of all is having a few special people give you a hand at just the right time."

In the fifth grade in Cleveland, Jesse met Charles Riley, an over-50-year-old white teacher and track coach who became his second father. Riley began mentoring Jesse in track and on life. "Coach Riley changed my life," Owens wrote.

"He was encouraging and supportive and really kind of looked out for my father," Rankin said.

Owens wrote that he tried to quell what Riley told him all champion athletes had to conquer: "The instinct to slack off, give in to the pain and give less than your best, and wish to win through things falling right, or your opponents not doing their best, instead of going to the limit, past your limit, where victory is always found."

Practice With Purpose

Owens worked to perfect simple, fundamental movements when running. "The best way to win (is) to run in as straight a line as possible," Owens wrote. "If you avoid excess motion, you can even beat a faster runner."

He leaned forward when running to cut wind resistance. He used his arms to help propel himself forward, but didn't let them cut across his chest. "This throws you off balance and creates a rocking motion that prevents you from driving ahead to the finish line," Owens wrote.

To win in competitions, Owens practiced with purpose. He made out weekly schedules. "I think that my success was partly because I followed (my routine) faithfully," he wrote.

Owens alternated easy days with hard ones, while keeping his practices short but effective.

"I believe that you can accomplish more in 45 minutes of practice if you work hard than you can in two hours if you don't train properly," he wrote.

Diligence paid dividends. In 1933, Owens broke the world record in the 220-yard dash. In 1935 at Ohio State, he broke three world records at the Big 10 Championships. His long jump of 26 feet, 8¼ inches, was a world record for more than 25 years. After breaking the world record in the 100-yard dash in 1936, he earned a spot on the U.S. Olympic team.

"In the early 1830s, my ancestors were brought to America as slaves for men who felt they had the right to own other men. In August of 1936, I battled with Adolf Hitler, . . . who thought all other men should be slaves to him and his Aryan armies," Owens wrote.

But on the track Owens put Hitler out of his thoughts and focused. "An angry athlete is an athlete who will lose every time," Owens recalled Riley telling him.

Owens won in the 100-meter dash, 200-meter dash and 400-meter relay. But in the long jump trials, he faltered. He fouled (stepping over the takeoff board) on his first attempt, and then fell short of the 24-foot, 6-inch qualifying distance on the second. With only one chance left for qualifying and seconds before he was required to jump, Owens felt the pressure.

Then, in a great display of sportsmanship, Luz Long, a German long jumper who'd set an Olympic record with his first qualifying jump, gave Owens a piece of advice.

Long suggested he concentrate solely on his jump, and to ensure he didn't foul, that he take off 6 inches before the takeoff board. Long had done the same thing the year before in a meet. Long even laid a towel right before the spot where he suggested Owens jump.

Owens listened when others had suggestions. He took Long's advice.

He also decided he needed to focus and relax. He took a deep breath, jumped and broke Long's record. Owens' 26-foot, 5⁵⁄₁₆-inch jump set an Olympic mark that lasted 24 years.

In spite of Hitler's racial hatred, Owens' determination won over the Berlin crowd. After he won the 100 meters and the long jump, the crowd chanted his name in admiration. In 1992, German officials honored Owens by renaming a street outside Olympic Stadium "Jesse Owens Strasse."

"It takes concentration and dedication to excel in sports," Owens said. "There are always diversions, . . . but if you want to excel in track and field, or anything else, you have to be willing to make some sacrifices. That's where discipline comes in."

17

Track Star
Wilma Rudolph

Focus And Sheer Grit Won Her
Three Olympic Gold Medals

Wilma Rudolph was 4 years old when she contracted polio. Doctors said she'd never walk again.

To make matters worse, Rudolph (1940–94) was a black child living in Clarksville, Tenn., in the 1940s. Her options for medical care were narrow. As the 20th of 22 children born to a railroad porter and a maid, Wilma also was poor.

Still, Wilma had a powerful force in her favor. Her mother, Blanche, decided she'd prove the doctors wrong.

Every week she took her daughter 45 minutes each way by bus to a Nashville hospital that agreed to give Wilma heat and water therapy for her leg. When that didn't help, doctors recommended daily massage. Her mother did it at home. When that didn't work, Blanche taught Wilma's brothers and sisters how to do the therapy and increased the massages to four times a day.

Just as important, she encouraged Wilma to use her legs as much as possible.

"My mother taught me very early to believe I could achieve any accomplishment I wanted to. The first was to walk without braces," Rudolph later said.

With hard work, Wilma finally graduated to a leg brace at age 8 and then to a special high-topped shoe.

Determined to improve her mobility, Wilma played basketball with her brothers every day. When they didn't have time for her, she played by herself.

One day, when Wilma was 11, her mother came home to find her daughter playing basketball outside in bare feet, the special shoe cast aside.

"'I can't' are words that have never been in my vocabulary," Rudolph would later say. "I believe in me more than anything in this world."

That fierce determination helped Rudolph in 1960 become the first American woman to win three gold medals in track in a single Olympics. In 1961, she won the James E. Sullivan Award, the top honor in the nation for amateur athletes. She was later inducted into the Black Athletes Hall of Fame and the Olympics Hall of Fame.

Powered By Inspiration

Throughout her youth, Rudolph continually challenged herself to improve. In high school, she began playing team basketball to keep her legs flexible. She found out what the records were for girls for the most points scored in one game and in a single season, and then broke them both.

Her skill gained the attention of Ed Temple, a track coach at Tennessee State University. Temple encouraged her to take up running. She got so good that in her junior year in high school, Temple invited her to try out for the Tigerbelles, the women's track team at Tennessee State.

On her first day of tryouts, Rudolph ran five miles through farmland, according to "Wilma Rudolph: Run for Glory" by Linda Jacobs. Rudolph fell several times, but made it to the finish line. On the second day, she was paired with one of the top Tigerbelles, who left Rudolph in the dust.

Injured and discouraged, Rudolph was sure she'd failed the tryout. But she refused to give up. She thought about all the work her family had put into helping her walk. Inspired, she went back the next day, tried again and won an invitation to join the team after she graduated from high school.

But she was still insecure and wondered aloud whether she would ever be as good as the other Tigerbelles.

"Quit wondering," her mother told her. "Work."

Rudolph followed her mother's advice. She used action to cure her fears. She ran so well during her senior year in high school that she qualified for the 1956 Olympics in Melbourne, Australia. She brought home a bronze medal in the women's 400-meter relay.

Rudolph kept raising the bar on her goals. She wanted to become one of the top Tigerbelles. To improve her running, she sought critiques from her teammates and coach.

"She was very coachable . . . even after three gold medals she would always listen," said Mae Faggs-Starr, a three-time Olympian and fellow Tigerbelle.

In 1959, Rudolph qualified for the 1960 Olympics in Rome by setting a world record in the 200-meter race. Once in Rome, she won gold medals in the 100-meter and 200-meter races.

Then a sprained ankle put in doubt Rudolph's entry in the 400-meter relay, in which she was to run the final leg. She wanted to win for her teammates, who were also Tigerbelles. She wanted to repay the people who'd helped her.

Rudolph summoned up all her will and focused on winning. Ignoring the pain in her ankle, she ran her heart out. The runner on the third leg made a bad baton handoff that let a rival pass Rudolph, but Rudolph came back to win, snagging a third gold medal.

Keep Striving

Charming and well-spoken, Rudolph became the darling of the 1960 Olympics. But she didn't rest on her laurels.

Because of her feats in the Olympics, Rudolph's hometown of Clarksville wanted to hold a parade and banquet in her honor. But Rudolph knew the event would be virtually all white. So she used her newfound hero status to challenge racial barriers.

Rudolph told organizers she wouldn't attend unless the celebration was integrated. The gambit worked. Her victory party was the town's first racially integrated event.

Although a hugely successful athlete, Rudolph always reminded herself to stay humble. "What do you do after you are world famous at 19 or 20 and have sat with prime ministers, kings and queens, . . . the pope? You come back to the real world," Rudolph wrote in her autobiography, "Wilma."

In the real world, track athletes had no professional circuit to join and weren't allowed at the time to make money as amateurs. So Rudolph retired from her sport at 22.

Instead of mourning the end of her running career, Rudolph shifted her goals. She decided that by becoming a teacher and coaching women's track teams, she could give young people a taste of the same support she experienced. In the classroom, she taught children that success meant reaching their own personal bests, not winning gold medals.

"When I was going through my transition of being famous, I used to ask God, 'Why was I here? What was my purpose?' Surely it wasn't just to win three gold medals," Rudolph wrote.

In 1982, she founded the Wilma Rudolph Foundation to help disadvantaged children learn about discipline, hard work and dedication in athletics and life. Rudolph said the foundation would be her greatest legacy. She died of brain cancer in 1994.

PART 3

Putting The "Work" In "Work Ethic"

Have a plan. Be committed. Get focused.

— NOLAN RYAN

18

Track Champion Carl Lewis

He Kept It Simple To Become One Of The Best

Carl Lewis isn't afraid to change — even when his old method seems to be working.

By 1996, Lewis had eight gold medals in track and field in three different Olympics to his credit. Although he was nearing 35 — old by Olympic standards — he wanted to make that year's U.S. Olympic team and compete in the Summer Games in Atlanta.

To do that, Lewis had to craft a plan. After scrutinizing his training methods, he made his decision: It was time to change.

"Forget how many times I'd already been to the Olympics. Forget the medals I'd already won. It was time to start all over again. And that would mean everything: new attitude, new diet, new fitness and training program," Lewis said in "One More Victory Lap," written with Jeffrey Marx.

"I still turn to one of my favorite quotes as an injection of fire," Lewis wrote. "'All athletes should bear in mind that they are competing not with other athletes but with their own capacities. Whatever I have already achieved, I have to go beyond,' and I will."

Because of his age and a back injury, Lewis knew he'd have to strengthen specific muscles. He began a weight-lifting program. Lewis had never lifted seriously. He'd been afraid that if he gained muscle, he'd sacrifice flexibility.

Facing down his fear, he went out and enlisted a top strength and conditioning coach. To maintain flexibility, he continued doing yoga, which he'd started a couple of years earlier.

Aware that he needed to be in prime shape, Lewis set out to fine-tune every aspect of his health. To combat allergies, he sought out a nutritionist. With supervision, he went on a six-week vegetarian cleansing diet.

For his work on the track, he relied on the guidance of Bob Tellez, his coach since 1979.

"I don't care who you are or how talented you might think you are — you better have a coach who knows what he's doing," Lewis wrote. "Anyone who wants to stay at the top of a sport — or a business — constantly needs to make adjustments."

He religiously followed his new training regimen. "I am executing this plan without wavering," he wrote at the time.

At the 1996 Olympic Games in Atlanta, Lewis won his ninth gold medal, this time in the long jump. His nine gold medals tie him with swimmer Mark Spitz and Finnish runner Paavo Nurmi for winning the most gold medals ever for a male athlete in the Summer Olympics. Lewis also won one silver medal.

He won a medal in all 10 Olympic events in which he competed, covering the Games in 1984, 1988, 1992 and 1996. He also was named to the U.S. team for the 1980 Moscow Olympics, which the U.S. wound up boycotting. He won gold medals in the 100-meter dash twice, the 200-meter dash once, the long jump four times and was on two winning 400-meter relay teams. His silver medal came in the 200-meter dash.

The Right Support

Lewis has long understood the need to enlist the help of others in any race for success.

"Surround yourself with experts," Lewis said in a 2000 interview. "No individual knows everything. So if you surround yourself with the best possible people (who) can give you the best knowledge and information, then you're going to have the best opportunity for success."

Maintaining mental flexibility is crucial for Lewis. "He's going to adapt . . . and evaluate as he goes along," Marx noted.

Yet when Lewis makes a decision and commits himself to seeing it through, it's a done deal. Such was his desire to be the best.

"Wanting to be the best that I could be was acceptable for a long time," Lewis said. "But when I saw I could be the best there was, then that's what became acceptable. And anything less than that is not being the best you can be.

"Be accountable for your choices, set your goals just beyond what you're sure of and never give up."

Lewis' most important principle? "Simplify your life," he said. For Lewis this means both personally and on the track.

During practice, Lewis and Tellez focused on executing a few simple, fundamental things. For example, when sprinting, Lewis concentrated and practiced first on simply "driving off the front block. If I do that well, everything else falls into place. You don't think about the competitor," said Lewis, who tries to "stay very relaxed" when running.

In the long jump, Lewis honed his approach. "For every practice long jump I took, I took 20 approaches." Most jumpers focus more on their jump than on their approach, he says.

Simplicity was golden for Lewis. "When we got to a meet, he was able to block out everything and only do what he was coached to do," Tellez said.

Lewis was born in Birmingham, Ala., in 1961, during the height of the civil rights movement, but moved two years later to Willingboro, N.J., where he grew up.

His parents, both track stars who became educators, knew the Rev. Martin Luther King Jr. and were active in the civil rights cause. Lewis wrote in his book "Inside Track," also with Jeffrey Marx, that he was "taught to speak up, and (was) educated about the civil rights movement my parents experienced firsthand."

He does speak up. Lewis refined his talent through fair play and hard work, and he's been an outspoken critic of athletes who cheat by using steroids. He was upset at having to compete against steroid abusers, but his main concern was the terrible message steroid use sent to youths.

"Kids are the key to the whole steroid issue. They have to realize that steroids can harm them and maybe even kill them," Lewis wrote.

"Carl stands up for what he thinks is right; that's the quality of a leader," said Joe Douglas, Lewis' manager since 1980.

Lewis transferred the values of study instilled in him by his teacher parents and applied them to his training. "You have to devote time and energy to something to expect to get something back from it," Lewis said.

Work Smart

He believes wholeheartedly in working smart. The "no pain, no gain mentality" is a particular pet peeve of his.

"Even for a professional athlete, I still don't buy into the theory of push, push, push until you drop. You need to be smarter than that," Lewis wrote.

A workout schedule, Lewis said, "should include hard, medium and easy days, and you should never have two hard days in a row." His motto: "Get the Rest, Do Your Best."

Being in shape, though, is only one of the keys to success in track, Lewis says.

"No matter what kind of physical shape you're in, you need plenty of practice, repetition after repetition. That's how you find your rhythm, and rhythm is what gives you the confidence to perform your best," he wrote.

"Carl has definite goals that he's set for himself. And whatever it's going to take to reach those goals (he'll do)," Tellez said.

For instance, when Lewis was in high school, he put the number 25 on his jacket to remind him of his goal to go 25 feet in the long jump.

"A lot of people laughed at me, telling me I was crazy to think I could jump that far," Lewis wrote.

He ignored the taunts. And he surpassed 25 feet several times in high school.

"I have always enjoyed creating challenges, going after them, making good on them," Lewis said. "I absolutely love pushing the limits and then seeing what happens. Always have. Always will."

19

Basketball Hall-Of-Famer Jerry West

His Dedication To The Game Made Him An NBA Legend

No matter how many games Jerry West played growing up in rural Cheylan, W.Va., the scenario was always the same. So were the participants.

Jerry West, the announcer, provided the details: "There are just two seconds left, and Jerry West has the ball."

Jerry West, the commentator, provided the color: "This is the kind of situation the young guard thrives on."

Jerry West, the ballplayer, faked right, faked left, jumped, shot and . . . hit the rim.

No matter. Jerry West was also the commissioner and could order the clock turned back. There'd be another final two seconds and another and another, until West made the shot and won the game.

"At an early age in my life, I was setting goals for myself," West said in 1999, "though I didn't realize it at the time. To me, to have goals is a reason to compete and excel. As I got older and read about successful people, I found a lot of them were setting goals for themselves at an early age."

Mr. Clutch

West's adult achievements exceeded even his fondest childhood dreams. He played for the Los Angeles Lakers for 14 years, from 1960 to 1974, and earned the nickname "Mr. Clutch." His teammates almost always put the ball in his hands when a game was on the line — and West usually won it for them.

He was selected to the all-star team each year he played, and was elected to the Basketball Hall of Fame. He was also named one of the 50 greatest players in the history of the game. West's silhouette is immortalized as the figure on the National Basketball Association's official logo.

After he retired as a player, he coached the Lakers for three years, from 1976 to 1979, and served the team as a consultant and general manager. West went on to become president of basketball operations for the Memphis Grizzlies.

The foundation of that success was laid in Cheylan, where he was born in 1938 and was one of six children in his family. The small community didn't have many organized activities. So West made up his own.

"You had to use your imagination to come up with ways to use your spare time," he said.

He'd spend as long as seven or eight hours a day on the courts. "I was always talking to myself, playing the role of game announcer and others," West said. "I could pretend to be anyone I wanted to be. I could have any success I wanted to have. I didn't feel I was going to be in a position where I was going to let myself fail."

By the time he got to high school, it had become obvious that he was more gifted than almost everyone else. But he refused to rely on natural talent. Instead, he continued to practice relentlessly.

"The thing that separates the average player from those perceived to be great is the instinctive part. But I don't think there's been a successful person who's played a sport who hasn't worked on it," West said.

In fact, West says his greatest strength as a player is that he refused to become complacent. He continued to work and practice, "and I got better every year."

As West played against better and better players, he found that he had to improve to keep up. Don't be afraid of competition, West says. Look for it.

In fact, one of the reasons today's athletes are so good is that even at the high school level they get invited to national and international tournaments and have the opportunity to play against the best. "Those kinds of experiences have to make you better," he said.

Some basketball players take pleasure in being outlandish. But there's nothing necessarily wrong with that, West says.

"Look at your own family; I'm sure your children are different from one another," West said. "So what — as long as everyone follows the same set of rules. I don't think you manage people. I think you work with people. Let everyone be different; let them have their own personalities. All these things are important to the team."

While he takes an active role in the team's management, he doesn't travel with the team itself. He doesn't want to hinder players' performances.

"I just don't think coaches and players want someone from management around all the time," he said. "I have a problem with hands-on managers in an organization. Why hire someone very competent and skilled and then tell them what to do and how to do it?"

That's not to say he doesn't set goals. He does that at the start of every season. But he keeps them to himself.

"I write down the number of games I think we should win, put it in an envelope and seal it," West said. "I don't look at it until the end of the season."

He uses that number as a benchmark that he reviews after the playoffs. Did the team meet the goal? Did the team exceed it? Why? Why not? The goals serve as both a check on past performance and a look at what the team needs for the future, West says.

Single-Minded Concentration

When West is concentrating on a goal, he focuses on it so closely he sometimes ignores the people around him.

For example, his wife, Karen, told *Sports Illustrated* that shortly after they were married, there was a three-week period when he didn't speak to her. Later he told her, "It's not personal. It's the playoffs."

When he makes a mistake, West reviews it carefully in his mind, looking for the cause. Once he finds it, he tells himself never to repeat that action.

A former teammate and roommate, Tommy Hawkins, remembers how after a bad night West would return to their room and replay the entire game. It was "a thorough recapitulation," Hawkins recalled.

But people shouldn't obsess over errors, either, West says. That kind of intensity is harmful. "If you never get away from the pressure, if you always feel you have to do better, always pushing the envelope, you just burn out.

"This is not about brain surgery," West said. "Most things are not. People sometimes take themselves too seriously in their job, and I don't think you can do that."

20

Golfer Tiger Woods
Constantly Striving To Improve
Has Propelled His Career

By the time Eldrick "Tiger" Woods was 6, he already played great golf. He often scored in the 90s on regulation courses, an amazing feat for someone so young.

Now it was time for him to gain a mental edge. His father and first golf coach, Earl Woods, tried to help him develop a winning attitude. If anybody could do it, Earl, a retired Army officer and former Green Beret, could. First, Earl bought the 6-year-old Tiger motivational and inspirational tapes to improve his confidence on the golf course.

Tiger listened repeatedly to them while swinging golf clubs in front of a mirror, putting on the carpet or watching videos of tournaments. He wrote down the tapes' messages and stuck them to his bedroom walls, studying them over and over. He imagined himself in all sorts of golf scenarios and applied the messages, which included:

"I will my own destiny. I believe in me. I smile at obstacles. I am firm in my resolve. I fulfill my resolutions powerfully. My strength is great. I stick to it, easily, naturally. My will moves mountains. I will focus and give it my all. My decisions are strong. I do it with all my heart."

Earl also went out of his way to annoy, harass or cheat Tiger when they played golf together. When Tiger was hitting a full wedge shot, Earl stood five yards in front of him and said, "I'm a tree." Tiger had to hit the ball over him.

While Tiger prepared to hit other shots, Earl jingled his change, pumped the brake on the golf cart, ripped the Velcro on his glove or rolled a ball in front of his son. Earl also marked his own shots closer to the hole than they should have been.

Although he'd get angry, Tiger knew his father was trying to help him improve. So he psyched himself up to overcome the distractions and to stay focused.

As a result, he mastered the art of concentration. Once, at a junior tournament, a marshal's walkie-talkie went off at its highest volume during Tiger's swing. He said he never heard it.

Tiger acquired mental toughness, a characteristic that has helped make him perhaps the best pro golfer today. He is now ranked No. 1 in the world, a mark that fluctuates based on points earned in tournaments.

After turning pro in September 1996 at age 21, he crafted one of the fastest starts in the history of pro golf. He posted a remarkable 40 PBA Tour wins, including eight majors, through early 2004. His career worldwide earnings of nearly $50 million were the highest in golf history.

All In His Head

Woods says it's critical that he keep a positive attitude. Case in point: his victory at the Motorola Western Open in Lemont, Ill., in July 1997.

"I won with my mind," he said. "I didn't drive the ball particularly well. My iron game was pretty good, and my putting came in spurts."

Woods despises losing. He won't accept it.

"That golf is not a life-or-death affair is a concept that has always eluded Woods," John Strege wrote in "Tiger: A Biography of Tiger Woods." "His approach to a match, particularly a match of historic significance, is that of a man who equates a loss with a mortal wound. When threatened with defeat, he will fight as though struggling for his life."

Woods is never content with his success and fame. He works incessantly to improve his skills.

On off days and after tournament rounds, he spends hours practicing his drives, iron shots, chipping and putting. If he shanks a drive or misses a putt, for example, he'll repeat the exercise until it's done perfectly.

He also strives to stay fit and get stronger. He jogs regularly, sometimes three miles at a time, to build up stamina. He lifts weights daily in a rigid program to add muscle to his arms and shoulders, a key reason he's one of golf's most powerful hitters.

Such determination is evident to golf legend Byron Nelson. "He's got that burning desire, the diligence never to let up," Nelson said. "In fact, I see his desire growing."

Woods has accomplished some amazing feats. He won six straight PGA Tour events in 1999–2000. The streak tied Ben Hogan's 1953 mark for second place in most consecutive PGA Tour victories. He also won the 1997 Masters with the lowest score (270) in the event's 61-year history.

Tiger's talent is rooted in his infancy. Earl, an avid golfer, put together a makeshift driving range for himself in the garage of the family's Cypress, Calif., home using a piece of carpet and a net. He hit balls over and over into the net as Tiger watched from his highchair. Tiger seemed to be studying the motion of Earl's swing.

Seeing his son's interest, Earl sawed off a golf club and gave it to Tiger. At 9 months old, he could strike the ball squarely into the net. At 18 months old, Tiger began going to local courses with Earl. Using his cut-down club, Tiger hit buckets of balls on the driving range.

When he was 4, Woods' father hooked him up with his first coach outside the family, Rudy Duran, a golf club professional.

On one occasion no more than a year later, Duran took Tiger to play on a tricky course in Costa Mesa, Calif. At the ninth hole, Tiger hit two shots that took him to the edge of a pond near the green. He contemplated how best to avoid the water.

"He decides how much of the lake he can cut off, (and) then hits it over to that side of the lake," Duran recalled. "Mozart composed finished music in his head. I saw that in Tiger. He was composing shots in his head."

Constant Challenge

Even as a tyke, Woods wanted to be challenged continually to keep improving. So in 1982, at the age of 6, he began entering junior tournaments.

He prepared carefully for each one, trying to figure out how to tailor his shots for the specific course.

Gradually, he came to dominate his competitors. He won the prestigious Optimist International Junior World tournament six times over the next decade. He also won a record three U.S. Junior Amateur championships and a record three U.S. Amateur titles, among a host of other events.

His confidence in his ability never wavered. After Woods said he wanted to study accounting in college, his father asked why.

"So I can manage the people who manage my money," he replied.

Woods enrolled at Stanford University in 1994 and played on the golf team for two seasons. He won the individual National Collegiate Athletic Association championship as a sophomore before leaving school and turning pro.

At least 85% of Woods' college wins came after he was even or trailing entering the final round, said Stanford coach Wally Goodwin. The coach attributes Woods' comeback ability to his mental toughness and bodily strength. Woods worked out every day and was "in better shape than anybody in college golf," the coach said.

He used that as a mental edge to intimidate the competition. "Everybody in college golf always heard him coming," Goodwin said. "They knew that if he wasn't leading, he was back there close and that he was a threat. That worked to their disadvantage and his advantage. They knew the guy was so tough."

21

Basketball Player
Jackie Stiles

Her Drive For Perfection
Helped Make Her The Nation's
No. 1 Scorer

To Jackie Stiles, practice breeds perfection. In her case, it made her the No. 1 scorer in women's college basketball history.

It's an approach Stiles began taking as a high school sophomore in 1994–95. Already a scoring machine, she was sidelined with a broken right wrist midway through the season. Doctors said she'd be out for more than a month.

Stiles immediately worried that her skills would deteriorate by the time she returned. The Claflin, Kan., native wanted to be the best, not a second-stringer.

With her right shooting hand in a cast, she went to the gym three days after the injury and began shooting left-handed. She wanted to develop a consistent shot with her opposite hand, but soon realized it wasn't working. So she ripped off the cast and decided to make her customary, right-handed shot even better.

Stiles thought the best way to learn was by doing. She'd park herself in the gym until she made — not just tried — 1,000 shots.

Several times a week, she shot sets of 200 shots from different spots on the floor. She confined herself to the gym as long as it took to reach the 1,000-made mark, which was sometimes way past midnight. She wore out the soles on pair after pair of her shoes. She kept in mind that success is a marathon, not a sprint, and that greatness would come.

She pursued the routine for her last 2½ years at Claflin High School. The strategy worked. Her shooting accuracy and point production escalated, and, by the end of her senior season in 1997, she was the No. 1 girls high school scorer ever in Kansas with 3,603 points.

Stiles stopped the 1,000-shot routine after high school. But she still challenged herself to be the best player she could be at Southwest Missouri State University.

She used the StairMaster for hours before practice. She was consistently the last one on the team to leave practice, staying late so she could work on jump shots, free throws and other factors of her game. While teammates were hitting the showers, she was still practicing. She never wanted to think she hadn't tried hard enough.

Her commitment paid off. She finished her college career with an all-time scoring mark of 3,393 points.

"I am driven; I hate to lose," Stiles said. "I want to get the most out of my talents and abilities. I never wanted to look back and say, 'If I would have done this. . . . What if I would have done that?'"

Stiles broke the record of 3,122 points by Mississippi Valley State's Patricia Hoskins in March 2001. It was anticipated all that season that she'd surpass Hoskins, and reporters peppered her with questions and flattering remarks en route to achieving the feat.

She didn't let the hype consume her. She never spoke about it with teammates and coaches out of concern that it might become a distraction. She handled the sequence with quiet determination and an eye toward keeping the team working together.

"Jackie is not the type of person who looks at the box score after the game to see how many more points she needs; she is totally the opposite," teammate Carly Deer once said. "She tried diverting (the attention) by concentrating on winning, not points."

Staying focused helped Stiles lead 29-6 Southwest Missouri State to the semifinals of the National Collegiate Athletic Association tournament. In one postseason game, a 60–53 upset victory over Rutgers, she played after sustaining a mild concussion two days prior. She scored 32 points, 17 in the final seven minutes.

Stiles could've sat out the game. But she knew her team needed her badly. "This is your senior year, and you go for it with everything you've got," she said.

Stiles' tournament performance capped a season in which she was the nation's leading scorer for the second time with a 31 per-game average. She also claimed Associated Press First Team All-American honors and was a finalist for the Naismith Award, which goes to the player of the year.

Stiles, 5-foot-8, directs her mind toward strategy. After a game, she reviews it mentally to check if there's something she could've done better.

"I can remember (when) I had 49 points against Northern Iowa this year, and I was like, 'Gosh, I missed those free throws,'" she said in 2001. "I've never played a perfect game."

When Stiles does something, she tries to do it well. On the court, she makes sure she has multiple skills to rely on. This requires extreme practice in addition to talent.

Experts note she can shoot from anywhere and make reverse spins and off-balance fadeaways, among other acrobatic shots. She's quick enough to create her own shot off the dribble. She knows, too, how to move without the ball and use screens in order to get open for a shot. She's also a great defensive player.

Throughout her basketball career, Stiles has been constantly the first option for her teams on offense. Even so, she doesn't try to win glory for herself. She often thinks pass first, shot second. She thinks that the more passes made, the better chance her squad has of shooting a high-percentage shot and scoring.

"I've had records in the past, and that's not what satisfies me," she said. "What drives me is team success and getting better as an individual to make the team better, doing whatever it takes to win games."

Off the court, she makes every effort to be gracious and act as a role model for girls.

"She'll stay an hour after the game just to make sure whoever wants an autograph or picture taken gets it," said Cheryl Burnett, who coached Stiles at Southwest Missouri State. "Jackie is a tremendous ambassador for women's basketball and athletics in general."

22

Iditarod Champ
Rick Swenson

His Determination Allowed Him
To Glide Ahead Of The Pack

The wind scratched at Rick Swenson's face. Snow came at him sideways like shards of frozen glass as he crossed from White Mountain to Nome, Alaska — the last 77 miles of the 1991 Iditarod Trail Sled Dog Race.

"There were times I couldn't even see the ground," Swenson recalled in a 2000 interview.

He was poised to take his fifth championship in the race. If he won, he'd break the record for the most Iditarod wins. First, though, he had to overcome this blizzard.

The wind chill factor was 100 degrees below zero. No one would've blamed him if he'd hunkered down in his sled bag and called it a night. But there was a catch, he said. "I wanted to win the Iditarod."

That meant inching toward his goal, no matter how slowly. One step at a time, as all the other racers turned back to wait out the storm, Swenson pushed his way into Nome to take the title, winning in a record 12 days, 16 hours and 34 minutes.

Swenson still holds the record for the most Iditarod wins. In March 2000, he competed in his 24th Iditarod, a dog-sled race that stretches 1,180 miles — the distance from Los Angeles to Seattle —

across Alaska's most rugged terrain, from Anchorage to Nome. He won the race in 1977, 1979, 1981, 1982 and 1991.

It started with a dream. In 1972, Swenson, then 22, told his family during Christmas dinner that he was moving to Alaska so he could run the Iditarod.

His family thought he'd read too many Jack London outdoor adventure stories.

Swenson learned to trap and fish growing up in Willmar, Minn., but he'd never been to Alaska. He didn't know anyone there. He knew how to ride a snowmobile and how to snowshoe. He'd raised a couple of pet dogs, but he didn't know much about teaching a group of canines how to pull him in a sled for more than 1,000 miles.

Still, Swenson was confident that if he set his mind to it, he'd be up to the challenge. Packing his bags, he left Minnesota in the fall of 1973. It was Alaska and the Iditarod or bust.

Learn From The Best

Swenson knew that experts could help him meet his goal. Before he left Minnesota, he wrote to Iditarod founder Joe Redington Sr.

Swenson picked Redington's brain by mail. He asked about dog breeds, sled types and weather patterns. He got some training tips from Redington, too, as well as a number of stories about the trail itself.

Redington's most useful advice? Stay on track and have faith in yourself. "(Redington) said, 'If you want to do something, then do it,'" said Kelly Williams, Swenson's kennel partner.

After Swenson reached Alaska, he visited Redington and bought a puppy from him. Redington introduced Swenson to other dog breeders. Soon, Swenson had a team of 12 young dogs.

Swenson knew he'd need a few years to toughen up and train himself and his team. To prepare for the rigors of the Iditarod, he moved into a cabin in the Alaskan bush, near Manley Hot Springs.

"The road was only open in the summertime, and there was no phone or no electricity," he recalled. To survive, he had to trap and hunt his food, haul water and cut wood to feed the cabin stove.

Swenson had his hands full. Not only did he have a team of wriggling dogs to manage, but he also had to make sure the wilderness didn't get the better of him.

How'd he do it? He focused his time by fitting training into his everyday life in the wild. When he needed to haul water or trap food, he'd hook the dogs to a sled to do so. If he had to pick up supplies in the winter, he rode his sled instead of using a snowmobile. Swenson worked with the dogs up to 16 hours a day as they figured out how to keep a tight tug on the sled.

He tried to prepare for any situation. He knew that if high winds and snow showers made trails invisible, he'd have to get in front of his lead dog and show it the way. To make sure he and the dogs worked as a team, he hiked on snowshoes and had the dogs follow him, so they'd learn to move together without getting tangled in their harnesses and wasting time.

His efforts paid off in 1977, when Swenson took his first victory. When the trail was snowed over, Swenson was able to proceed without delay by leading his dogs, tangle-free, for 50 miles.

Indoor Analysis

Swenson found a way to prepare even when he was indoors. He studied his dogs' behavior, watching them through his cabin's picture window. While he ate his meals or mended his gear indoors, he zeroed in on the activities of the dogs outside.

He learned about their personalities. He figured out how they got along with each other, what kind of food they liked, which was patient, which was quick to anger and which the others followed. By gathering as much information as he could on his dogs before the event, Swenson was better able to control them during the race.

Swenson's goal in the beginning was to finish one Iditarod. By 1976, he'd prepared so well he placed 10th in his first race — an outstanding finish for a rookie. But he wasn't satisfied — he wanted to be the best.

Once he made it through his first race, Swenson honed his psychological edge.

"(Swenson) would have a certain way (of) psyching somebody out, maybe getting them off their schedule by just a comment he might make," said Greg Bill, director of development for the Iditarod. Swenson would sometimes encourage other racers to speed up and catch a racer down the road. In the meantime, he'd rest his dogs, catch up and then leave them all in the dust.

Other racers learned to watch out for Swenson's poker face. They also respected him for keeping them on their toes. His tricks taught them lessons that made them better.

"(Swenson) toughened me by fire," three-time Iditarod champion Martin Buser told *Outside* magazine. Over the years, Swenson faced a host of fierce opponents. But his rivalry with four-time champ Susan Butcher made the most headlines. As she nabbed titles in 1986, 1987, 1988 and 1990, it seemed she'd out-do Swenson.

Swenson used the pressure of close competition to improve his technique. "(Rivalry) enables you to reach deeper, throw farther and work harder," he said.

Rivalry was only part of what spurred him to charge through the blizzard during the 1991 contest.

He was determined to win his fifth race.

As he braced himself and led his dogs where the trail had disappeared, he kept himself motivated by repeating his slogan, "Never turn back."

"He was as smart as anyone on the trail and mentally tougher," wrote Jon Larson, a member of the committee that named Swenson to the Iditarod Hall of Fame in 1997. "He won because he willed it."

23

Julius "Dr. J" Erving

Never Being Satisfied Made Him
One Of Basketball's Greatest

It was the spring of 1974, and Julius Erving had just led the New York Nets to their first American Basketball Association championship. Dr. J, as he is known, also just won the league's Most Valuable Player Award.

You'd think Erving would spend the summer laying in a hammock and smelling the roses. But that wasn't the basketball all-star's approach. Dr. J always wanted to improve himself.

He was never satisfied with his level of play. He planned to spend the off-season learning how to play the game even better. "I want to learn to play defense differently from now on," he said during a press conference. "I want to be more physical. To lean on a man. Wear him down.

"Defense is where games are won and lost in the pros. There are a lot of guys on our team who can score 20 (points). If I can play physical defense, I can help the team. Of course, I still want the guys to depend on me when we need the big points."

Erving's efforts paid off. He's in the Basketball Hall of Fame and a member of the National Basketball Association's All-Time Team. He's considered by some to be the reason the NBA finally agreed to a merger with the American Basketball Association. As *Sports Illustrated* noted: "If Erving didn't actually force the 1976 ABA-NBA merger, he was surely the most valuable asset the young league brought to the table."

Erving was born on Feb. 22, 1950, in Hempstead, N.Y. His father left the family when Julius was 3 years old. His mother, who worked long hours as a domestic to support the family, raised him alone.

Ticket Out

At an early age, Erving realized that basketball could be a ticket to a better life. He had a natural talent on the court. So he honed his athletic ability while studying hard. His good grades and basketball skill earned him a scholarship to the University of Massachusetts.

Erving knew his weaknesses and worked hard to eliminate them. According to "The Legend of Dr. J" by Marty Bell, Erving began a self-improvement program almost the day he arrived at college.

"He was a rough playground player. He was a poor outside shooter. But he recognized his limitations," Bell wrote. "In the late summer heat of September, he would go down to the gym and work on his game. It was 90 degrees inside, and you couldn't wear anything but shorts. But Julius would work for hours by himself."

He also knew he couldn't win by himself. So Erving worked to become the ultimate team player, ready to sacrifice personal statistics. The "coaches used a team-oriented game that emphasized defense and set plays on offense. They did not change their style for Julius. Rather than adopting a wide-open, run-and-shoot schoolyard attack, they asked him to learn the discipline of their theories," Bell wrote. "He adjusted quickly."

Erving's time at school coincided with the battle between the fledgling ABA and the established NBA. It was the first time a professional basketball league drafted underclassmen. Erving left UMass at the end of his junior year to play with the Virginia Squires (1971–73), the Nets (1973–76) — with whom he won his first two league titles — and finally the Philadelphia 76ers (1976–87), with whom he won another title.

Erving was a gifted player. He fine-tuned his natural abilities by studying the game and his opponents. "I was only 6-foot-3 when I graduated from high school," Erving said. "And yet I always had the big hands and could jump, so I learned to be trickier than the bigger guys.

"I like to experiment. I love to watch guys and what they'd do in an emergency situation. When I practiced, I worked on ways to take advantage of my advantages."

He also refused to limit himself to one style of play. That way, he said, "I could do anything that I had ever seen any guy do."

Erving knows the value of setting goals. To make sure he reached greatness, the goals he set were big ones.

"It wasn't until I was 14 or 15 that I first heard about the Pulitzer Prize. And I started thinking about this. I always liked poetry, and I always liked writing. At that age I made a declaration to my family that I was going to win the Pulitzer Prize one day," Erving told the Academy of Achievement.

"Of course I never did, and probably never will. But I think that was pretty much evidence of thinking big, thinking with a more universal perspective than one's neighborhood or one's city, state or even country."

Looking For Role Models

For inspiration, he read biographies, particularly those written about black Americans, people who could serve as "role models in terms of achievers."

As Erving achieved fame, he tried not to take himself too seriously, not to believe the compliments of the sycophants who surround successful people. "I started to understand the insincerity of someone coming up and saying, 'You're the greatest' and 'You're the best,' and saying the same thing to someone else down the street," he said.

It's also crucial to honestly consider your skill levels, Erving said.

"Take the time to assess your talent yourself, and then be willing to listen to others who can tell you what you have," he said. "Just deal with the reality of the situation."

His levelheadedness, desire to improve, work ethic and skills made him a leader on the court.

"I think people see commitment," he said. "I think as a youngster the work ethic was there, practicing hard, being dedicated and not by nature being a complainer."

24

Running Back
Walter Payton

Determination Helped Him Run
Over The Competition

After his second season with the Chicago Bears, pro football player Walter Payton knew one thing: "The only way you can perform is to prepare and condition yourself."

Keeping a practice regimen he began while a teen-ager in Columbia, Miss., he ran up a hill — repeatedly.

In Arlington Heights, Ill., near his Lake Forest home, he found his hill — 80 yards high at a 45-degree angle.

The first time he and some of his teammates tried it, they could run it only twice. "But by the time it was time to report to training camp, we could run it 25 times," he told cable sports network ESPN.

Running the hill and a rigorous weight-training program underscored the famous running back's determination. He wanted to be the best he could be.

By the time his 13-season pro football career ended in 1987, he was the best running back ever.

Payton, who died in 1999 of liver cancer at age 45, holds or co-holds seven National Football League records. He was also the former NFL record holder of the most yards rushing in a career (16,726). He went to the Pro Bowl nine times and was the NFL's Player of the Year in 1977 and 1985. He was elected into the Hall of Fame in 1993.

Not Just Natural Talent

Born in Columbia, Payton came to football later than most boys. His devout Baptist parents didn't want him to play football like his older brother Eddie, also an NFL player, until Walter reached high school. In fact, he didn't go out for the team until his junior year.

Still, his natural ability was clear from the outset. The first time he carried the ball, he ran 60 yards for a touchdown.

But he knew ability alone wouldn't carry to him to the top. He had to work hard. To train, he found his first hill, a levee on the Pearl River. He built a 65-yard course, pushing himself to develop his stamina and his leg strength.

They served him well, both at nearby Jackson State University and in the pros. He set several college records, including the all-time college scoring mark. He was the Chicago Bears' first draft pick — fourth overall — after graduating in 1975.

He didn't rest on his college achievements. Even though he was slowed by an elbow injury in his rookie year with the Bears, he vowed to do everything he could to help the team.

"If you keep on fighting, keep your focus, you will always win," he said in an interview in 1987 with ESPN.

In addition to running the hill, he lifted weights almost religiously.

"He's been a great person to me in teaching you how to be the best you can be at anything," former defensive end Richard Dent told the *Chicago Tribune*. Teammate and guard Revie Sorey agreed. "He worked twice as hard as we did."

Bears conditioning coach Clyde Emrich recalled that Payton could lift a 100-pound dumbbell with one hand.

The drive to excel came from within, for the Bears were mediocre during much of Payton's career. But that never stopped him from staying focused on his goal of always improving.

"If you can visualize what you want to do, you can do it," he told Roy Firestone of ESPN.

"I look(ed) at tape(s) of myself," he said in a 1981 interview with the *Tribune*, "not to see what I did on a play, but what I could do to make it better. There are too many has-beens who got that way by looking back and getting satisfied."

On the field, Payton was rarely satisfied. He's remembered as much for his willingness to hit defenders as he was for his elusive leg action.

He didn't run out of bounds at the end of a play, preferring instead to "punish," in the words of several teammates and opponents, a tackler.

"It's not a matter of pride; it's a matter of survival, because if you let those guys beat up on you, you won't be in there too long," he told the *Tribune* once.

But to Payton, succeeding depended on more than just physical toughness.

"I wasn't the biggest or the fastest or the strongest," the 5-foot-10, 205-pound Payton told ESPN, "but I was the smartest." He would watch films of opponents until he knew defenders' habits inside and out. He would often say that football was a game of angles. "If you can figure out the angles, you've got the edge."

He also reasoned that most leg injuries come from being hit when the leg is bent too much. So he developed a more straight-legged style, trying never to let his knees bend more than 30 degrees. Other backs' knee angles when running averaged closer to 90 degrees.

His reasoning paid off. He missed only one game in his pro career and was irked at having to do so. He blamed his coaches for overreacting to an ankle injury.

He also learned from everyone he could.

"You look at a Pete Rose to be the terrific athlete he is, and then he falls on hard times," Payton said in his acceptance speech for the NFL Hall of Fame. "But when he played the game, I got something from the way he played the game, because he hustled every play, and just because he had one mistake in his life, am I supposed to throw back everything that I gained from him?"

Criticism Spurred Him On

"There is one thing that can get me angry before the game. If I hear fans say something like, 'You won't do anything today, Payton,' then I really get mad. I don't like people telling me I can't do something."

That determination had a lighter side as well. A practical joker, he kept his teammates loose with antics that included walking 50 yards on the sidelines on his hands.

That attitude made a difference to his teammates. Coach Mike Ditka faced a team split into factions. Ditka said Payton's upbeat outlook helped him form a bridge between the two camps.

"He was the one guy who really worked hard at pulling that team together in the 1980s, when it could have come apart. We were kind of in factions of offense and defense, and he really worked hard at pulling it together. He got each side to respect each other, and we finally became a football team instead of an offense and defense," Ditka told the *Tribune*. The Bears won Super Bowl XX following the 1985 season.

Despite his achievements, Payton was modest with his teammates and the media. He said in 1977, "I'm not a star. People who don't know much about football say I'm a star. It's important to me to just be one with my teammates."

Even as he faced death from cancer caused by a rare liver disease, he stayed positive.

"He didn't ask, 'Why me?'" said teammate Mike Singletary, who visited Payton the day before he died. "He continued to look forward to what he could do to help his family."

25

Pitcher Nolan Ryan

His Focus Gave Batters
5,714 Reasons To Worry

Nolan Ryan threw hard — his fastball was often timed at more than 100 miles per hour. But the reason he dominated batters had as much to do with his mind-set as it did with his right arm.

"You're not going to get very far until you have a burning desire to excel," wrote Ryan in "Miracle Man: Nolan Ryan, The Autobiography," with Jerry Jenkins.

For Ryan, desire translated into preparation. "Mental discipline and intense focus on what you're doing begin early in a pitcher's day," he wrote. "Before each start, I sit in the clubhouse and analyze the other team's hitters. I concentrate on visualizing what I've done in the past to get a hitter out. . . . It's a pregame ritual that reinforces the fact that I'm mentally prepared to pitch effectively."

Ryan studied his opponents so he could take advantage of their weaknesses. "There's more to pitching than just heading out to the mound and throwing strikes. All hitters, even the great ones, have their weaknesses. It's up to a pitcher to discover and exploit a hitter's flaws," he wrote in "Nolan Ryan's Pitcher's Bible," with Tom House.

Over a major-league record 27-year career (1966–93), the combined batting average for opposing hitters against Ryan was a paltry .204. His seven career no-hitters and 5,714 strikeouts are major-league records by a wide margin. Ryan won 324 games and was elected to the Baseball Hall of Fame in 1999.

Branching Out

The key to Ryan's longevity had its roots in 1972, when he was a struggling 25-year-old flame-thrower with a mediocre record.

Ryan had just been traded from the New York Mets to the California Angels when he discovered a weight room at the Angels' home park of Anaheim Stadium. It wasn't there for the baseball team. The common belief back then was that weight training was bad for baseball players because it made them muscle-bound and robbed them of needed flexibility. Pitchers were to get their conditioning solely from running.

"But I felt that there had to be more a pitcher could do to maintain his stamina and strengthen his upper body; by using weights, I believed I'd be a better-conditioned athlete," Ryan said. "So I basically just started lifting, experimenting with different exercises to see what kind of results I'd get."

He began what eventually became a sophisticated weight-training regimen that lasted his entire career and was tailored to his needs. "Anything that doesn't go into making you a better pitcher ought to be cut out of your regimen. Have a plan. Be committed. Get focused," Ryan said.

"There's no doubt in my mind that if it hadn't been for that weight room, I would have been out of the game many years ago," he added. "Once you fatigue, it affects your mechanics, (and) you can no longer pitch with the precise timing required for a smooth, compact motion."

In 1989, at the age of 42 — ancient in baseball — Ryan's 301 strikeouts made him the oldest man ever to strike out 300 batters in a season. Ryan pitched his sixth and seventh no-hitters when he was 43 and 44.

"Through physical conditioning, a good diet and the right attitude, you can actually slow down the aging process," he said. "You can't deter the body from aging, but you can slow the pace at which it ages."

"There's nobody that ever worked harder at keeping himself in shape than Nolan did," said Jim Fregosi, who managed Ryan in 1978–79. "He was a perfectionist. He wanted to be perfect in everything he did."

On the mound, Ryan was a study in concentration. "Maintaining concentration depends on what I call tunnel vision; nothing else in the world exists but the catcher's target, the hitter and my perfect delivery," Ryan said. "It requires incredible concentration to get the location I want on every fastball. I can't let up — even for a second."

When things didn't go Ryan's way, he refused to get rattled. "If it seems as if everything is going against you . . . just step off the mound, take a deep breath and think about what you're doing — allow yourself enough time to regroup," he said. "I really believe in that. Don't get so wrapped up in the emotional end of things that you lose direction; remember, never let the failure of your last pitch affect the success of your next one.

"You can't have a successful career without a positive attitude. I believe that an 'I can do this' mentality is a pitcher's best friend."

Professional Approach

When Ryan was traded to the Angels after the 1971 season, he hadn't had one outstanding year in his five seasons. So he sought out expert advisers in the Angels' spring training: catcher Jeff Torborg and pitching coach Tom Morgan. Torborg helped Ryan learn to stop overthrowing. Morgan helped Ryan develop a controlled, more compact delivery.

The result: a solid 1972. He had 19 wins, an earned-run average of 2.28, nine shutouts and 329 strikeouts in 284 innings.

"Nolan had so much drive and was such a willing worker. He worked as hard as any human being could," said Torborg, who caught Ryan's first no-hitter.

"Nolan believed in himself," said Art Kusnyer, who as an Angel caught Ryan's second no-hitter. "He knew if he kept pushing it, if he kept working at his delivery, that he was going to become more consistent. He always wanted to be better, and always wanted to compete at the highest level."

Ryan also made sure he behaved at that level. "He was an ultimate professional," said former Angel play-by-play announcer Dick Enberg. "Baseball players, especially in that era (the 1970s), had a reputation of playing hard on the field and playing hard off the field. I think every team had their fair share of really talented players who weren't necessarily professional away from the field. Nolan Ryan was."

Knowing that consistency is crucial, Ryan worked to be reliable every time he stepped on the mound, Enberg said. "You knew he'd be out there every fourth day, you knew even if he threw 150 pitches he'd still be out there. He was ready to pick up the ball and do his job."

Ryan believes in mastering his craft. "Learn the game by studying it. Know what separates the average player from the good player," he said. "The answer is that it was their hearts and their drive and their intellects. They wanted to become the best ballplayers they could, so they put in extra work. They put in the time on fundamentals, played to their strengths and worked on their weaknesses."

Even with all of his fame, Ryan keeps his focus on what is most important to him: his wife, Ruth, and their three children. "All the no-hitters wouldn't mean anything without my family being there to support me. I think you need to seek a sense of balance in your life," he said.

"Because of the way I was raised I always believed that no matter how successful you are, it should not change you as a person. It doesn't entitle you to treat people any differently than if you were just another person trying to make a living. I believe I should treat the fan in the bleachers the same way I would treat the president — with respect."

Alan Ashby, who with the Houston Astros caught Ryan's fifth no-hitter, said: "Nolan certainly was given the gift of drive. And it showed up in his work ethic. He was just a guy who was driven to be the best he could be."

26

Lance Armstrong Rides To Win

Cycling Champ Races Ahead With Hard Work And Determination

There are no lucky socks in Lance Armstrong's suitcase. He doesn't drink raw eggs before workouts. You'll never hear him chanting.

And when he gave motivational talks to employees at Interwoven Inc., a Sunnyvale, Calif.–based software company and one of his sponsors, Armstrong didn't dole out visualization techniques or success acronyms.

"If there were any advice, it would be, 'Go back to work,'" said Brad Kearns, director of corporate programs at Interwoven, in a 2001 interview.

Kearns is a longtime friend of Armstrong who used to compete against him in the triathlon, a sport combining running, cycling and swimming, in the days before Armstrong became a professional cyclist.

"He's completely devoid of superstition. I asked him further about that, and he's like, 'I just don't have use for that, because all I need to know is I've worked harder than the next guy,'" Kearns said. "It's very cut and dried and simple and mechanical for him."

Riding on the U.S. Postal Service Cycling Team, Armstrong won the Tour de France, a prestigious three-week, 2,290-mile bicycle race in France, five years in a row — from 1999 through 2003. In 2003, The Associated Press named him Athlete of the Year.

How'd he do it? "I rode when no one else would ride, sometimes not even my teammates," the Austin, Texas, resident wrote in his bestselling book, "It's Not About the Bike: My Journey Back to Life," co-authored by Sally Jenkins.

"I remember one day in particular, May 3 (1999), a raw European spring day, biting cold. I steered my bike into the Alps, with (team director Johan Bruyneel) following in a car. By now it was sleeting and 32 degrees. I didn't care. We stood at the roadside and looked at the view and the weather, and Johan suggested that we skip it. I said, 'No. Let's do it.' I rode for seven straight hours, alone. To win the Tour I had to be willing to ride when no one else would ride."

In 1993, Armstrong burst onto the international scene by winning the World Road Race Championship in Oslo, Norway. He then won the Tour DuPont in 1995 and 1996 and competed in the 1996 Olympics.

Cancer Strikes

In October 1996, less than a month after his 25th birthday, he was diagnosed with testicular cancer. With the help of top-notch physicians and a good dose of resolve, Armstrong fought back. In October 2001, he celebrated five years since his cancer diagnosis, and he is considered by doctors to be cured.

Shortly after he won the 1999 Tour, critics accused Armstrong of taking performance-enhancing drugs. Some even said his chemotherapy gave him an edge.

He proved himself by testing clean over and over. His response: "Everybody wants to know what I'm on. What am I on? I'm on my bike busting my ass six hours a day."

Armstrong learned the power of elbow grease by example. His mother, Linda, was a single mom who made ends meet. She taught Armstrong to get off the couch if he wanted to succeed.

"She's sharp as a tack, and she'll outwork anybody," Armstrong said. While raising Lance, Linda Armstrong climbed the ladder from secretary to account manager at the Texas offices of Ericsson, the Swedish telecommunications company.

"Sometimes she would talk about how frustrated she was at work, where she felt she was underestimated because she was a secretary," Armstrong said. " 'Why don't you quit?' I asked. 'Son, you never quit,' she said. 'I'll get through it.' "

Armstrong remembered that. It came in handy when he started racing professionally back in 1992. In his first pro race, the San Sebastian Classic in Spain, Armstrong finished dead last — 111th out of 111.

"Fifty riders dropped out, but I kept pedaling," Armstrong said. "I crossed the finish line almost half an hour behind the winner, and as I churned up the last hill, the Spanish crowd began to laugh and hiss at me. 'Look at the sorry one in last place,' one jeered."

Armstrong thought about giving up the sport. Then he recalled what Mom always told him — never quit. He got back on the bike for his next race.

To stay focused, Armstrong sets long- and short-term goals. "I generally determine my major goals a year in advance," he wrote in his book "The Lance Armstrong Performance Program."

"I realize that there are many variables outside of my control in my quest, but focusing on a big goal down the road really motivates me. To help me stay focused, I set micro-goals such as races or training achievements that bring me one step closer to being at my best for my major goals."

Setting goals actually helped Armstrong fight cancer. At one point, he was given less than a 50% chance of survival. Visualizing benchmarks — and then meeting them — kept his hope alive through four rounds of chemotherapy and risky brain surgery to remove cancerous lesions.

"I began to set goals with my blood (counts), and I would get psyched up and meet them," he said. "(Physicians) would tell me what they hoped to see in the next blood test, say a 50% drop (in markers that indicate the presence of cancer). I would concentrate on that number, as if I could make the counts by mentally willing it."

Make Your Own Luck

Armstrong's motto: You make your own luck. Early in his career, folks told him he'd never make it as a competitive cyclist. "When he quit triathlons and signed up for cycling, I said, 'Lance, that was the biggest mistake you've ever made in your life,'" Kearns said.

Armstrong proved them wrong.

He focused on the power of positive thinking. Through cancer, Armstrong says, he developed the patience and long-range thinking he needed to win the Tour. Cancer taught him a lot of things he might never have learned otherwise. In fact, he insists, he's grateful for the C-word.

"The truth is that cancer is the best thing that ever happened to me," he said. "I don't know why I got the illness, but it did wonders for me, and I wouldn't want to walk away from it. Why would I want to change, even for a day, the most important and shaping event in my life?"

27

Wrestler And Coach Dan Gable

Hard Work And Focus Helped Make Him The Greatest Wrestler Of The Century

For legendary amateur wrestler and coach Dan Gable, mental breaks are necessary. But don't suggest to him that he take a long vacation to relax.

"I can get the same thing out of reading a good fishing magazine," he said in a 2001 interview. "My mind's never gone very far away from what I wanted to accomplish."

This relentless focus, combined with immense physical ability, helped make Gable the best wrestler of the 20th century, say experts.

Gable earned every major championship available to an American wrestler, including the 1972 Olympic gold medal. He lost just one match in his wrestling career.

He retired from coaching in 1997 with an impressive 355-21-5 dual-meet record, 15 National Collegiate Athletic Association team trophies and 45 individual championships.

Pumped-Up Values

It all started at the YMCA in Gable's hometown of Waterloo, Iowa. First a competitive swimmer, Gable left the water for the mat after his first wrestling experience.

"I liked the feeling that you get," he said. "You can't replicate it anywhere else."

Today, Gable cites the Y's influence. "It's not the playground. It's an organized setting where people are teaching you values."

Gable also learned values from his parents, iron-willed Mack, owner of a real estate company, and no-nonsense Katie. Gable's parents insisted on two responses when their children encountered others: They had to be respectful, and any comment they made had to be positive.

"It didn't even have to be right," he said. "I just soaked it right in."

Les Anderson, a two-time NCAA champion who coached Gable at Iowa State University, said Gable was the easiest and best wrestler he ever worked with. "The reason for that is, No. 1, his intelligence, and No. 2, his intense desire not to lose, which was far more important than a desire just to win," he said in "A Season on the Mat" by Nolan Zavoral.

Gable's only loss occurred when he was a senior at Iowa State during the 1970 NCAA 142-pound final in Evanston, Ill., against Larry Owings.

"At the end of the match, there was a referee's call that really wasn't a clear call. The decision went the other way — against me — four points against me," Gable said.

While Gable admitted that loss was still painful, he said it had a purpose. "That match was good to me. It brought my mentality up, my goals up. It made me better," he said.

The specific lesson he learned was never to hand over a match to the referee, to always dominate from the moment the match began — and even before. "I wanted to make sure that if I was capable of winning, that I was winning by that nth degree," Gable said.

To reach that degree, Gable intensified his workouts. He didn't need a clock to tell him when a practice was over. His body did.

"I always wanted to push myself to the point of exhaustion, collapse," he said. Often, Gable worked so hard he had to crawl toward the gym door until he could gather enough strength to stagger out.

In practice, Gable was known for taking on any willing opponent, even his more-than-400-pound Iowa State and Olympic teammate Chris Taylor. Gable was so fiercely intent on winning that he simply wouldn't quit, said Taylor, who died in 1979.

"I can do pretty good with (Gable) for about the first 30 minutes," Taylor said. "After that, he tires me out and I can't do anything."

For Gable, getting the mental game back after his single loss required some internal positive feedback. At his very next meet — the Amateur Athletic Union Championships of 1970 — Gable won three matches for a combined score of 25–1.

"There's nothing like success. If I had not won, or even not done a good job, I might have squandered my career." Instead, Gable said, "I got that surge."

In Munich in 1972, Gable rolled to a gold medal in freestyle wrestling at 149.5 pounds, preventing a single point from being scored against him — an unheard of and astounding achievement for the sport.

Goal Getter

After the Olympics, Gable wanted to help others achieve greatness as well. He joined the University of Iowa's coaching staff to do so. There he continued boosting his goals.

When he found he could coach a team to a championship, he started working toward creating a champion in every weight class.

"There's always ways of motivating yourself to higher levels. Write about it, dream about it," Gable said. "But after that, turn it into action. Don't just dream."

Gable does more than dream. He puts things down on paper. "I fill notebooks," he said. "It keeps everything in front of me often. It reminds me so I'm more likely to get it done."

Those reminders are vital, Gable says, because the environment is constantly changing. "I don't stay with the old; I go with the new," he said.

While many coaches plan their team's practices week by week, Gable was more likely to change things when needed, even mid-practice. "I can understand how (coaches) plan. I can't understand how they stay with it," he said.

It's the same with individual wrestlers. Gable said it takes time to find what motivates each one. "You keep searching and searching, and eventually you come up with it — you find that button," he said. Pushing the right button helps "get inside your kid's head to the point that they totally believe what you're saying."

The hardest thing he had to teach? "Sustaining effort is very difficult," Gable said. So he kept after his wrestlers with verbal pushes. During a 1997 workout, for instance, Gable yelled to his wrestlers: "You hit the wall after a match! When you sit down, that's when you hit the wall. You get tired then!"

Gable continued to influence collegiate wrestlers as an assistant to the University of Iowa's athletic director. He also traveled the country doing motivational speeches.

Gable had found a way to motivate listeners. He used a graph to illustrate his approach to life's peaks and valleys. "My valleys are higher than most people's peaks," he said. "I stay at that level."

28

Babe Ruth Grew To Greatness

Shedding A Poor Childhood, He Became Baseball's Sultan Of Swat

For George Herman "Babe" Ruth, greatness meant no fear. When the Boston Red Sox traded Ruth to the New York Yankees in 1920 and he switched to the outfield full time (he'd been a dominant pitcher), striking out at the plate was still considered an embarrassment for a batter. The game was emerging from the "dead ball" era, and batters feared a poor showing at the plate.

The power-hitting Ruth (1895–1948) saw things differently. "Never let the fear of striking out get in your way," he said.

For years Ruth held the career strikeout record, whiffing 1,330 times (since surpassed by a wide margin by many players). But he dominated the game like no other batter, with the possible exception of Barry Bonds.

When Ruth retired in 1935, he was baseball's all-time home run king with 714, and its all-time runs batted in leader with 2,204. He still holds the highest career slugging percentage — total bases divided by at bats — at .690. In addition, Ruth's career batting average was a lofty .342.

Rather than let home runs come naturally, as some of the game's great home run hitters have, Ruth vigorously sought them out.

"I swing as hard as I can, and I try to swing right through the ball," Ruth said. "In boxing, your fist usually stops when you hit a man, but it's possible to hit so hard that your fist doesn't stop. I try to follow through the same way. The harder you grip the bat, the more you can swing it through the ball, and the farther the ball will go. I swing big, with everything I've got. I hit big or I miss big. I like to live as big as I can."

The Benefits Of Change

His excesses off the field are as legendary as his feats on it. He enjoyed the nightlife so much that a former roommate, Ping Bodie, was quoted as saying, "I don't room with him. I room with his suitcase."

Yet Ruth knew when it was time to change course. In his younger days, being out of shape and overweight didn't prevent him from dominating the game. Then his lifestyle caught up with Ruth during the 1925 season. He reported to camp at his heaviest weight, 250 pounds, and responded with his worst season — a .290 batting average and just 25 home runs. Even worse, Ruth, who'd been on four championship teams, watched his Yankees tumble to seventh place.

Ruth was honest with himself and took personal responsibility for his failings. "I'm going to make good all over again. I used to get sore when people called me a sap and tried to steer me right," he said. "But all those people were right. Now, though, I know that if I am to wind up sitting pretty on the world, I've got to face the facts and admit that I have been the sappiest of saps."

For the first time in his career, Ruth committed to a training regimen in the off-season. He joined a gymnasium and worked out almost daily. He practiced his swing religiously.

When he reported to spring training in 1926, his weight was down to 212 pounds. Ruth was in "the best shape he had been in since his early years with the Red Sox," wrote Robert Creamer in "Babe: The Legend Comes to Life."

Ruth rebounded with a .372 average, 47 home runs and 145 RBIs. The next year, for the legendary 1927 Yankees, Ruth hit .356 with 60 home runs and 164 RBIs while leading the team to a World Series title. He was dubbed the Sultan of Swat.

"Despite his big belly, which waned and waxed through the years like the moon, he was never again seriously out of shape," Creamer wrote. "From 1926 through 1931 — as he aged (from 31 to 36) — Ruth put on the finest sustained display of hitting that baseball has ever seen. During those six seasons, he averaged 50 home runs a year, 155 runs batted in and 147 runs scored; he batted .354."

Ruth looked at his time at the plate as a war of wills. Playing in an era before batting helmets and when pitchers thought nothing of backing a hitter off the plate by throwing a fastball at his head, Ruth refused to be intimidated.

"He was very brave at the plate," former major-league player and Hall of Fame manager Casey Stengel said. "You rarely saw him fall away from a pitch. He stayed right in there. No one drove him out."

Making A Difference

Although Ruth — who played on seven world championship teams — received enormous individual attention for his feats, he understood and pushed for teamwork on the field.

"The way a team plays as a whole determines its success," he said. "You may have the greatest bunch of individual stars in the world, but if they don't play together, the club won't be worth a dime," he said.

Ruth believed in lending a hand where he could. Take his monetary generosity. While he was the highest-paid player of his era by far (making as much as $80,000 a year in 1930–31), he often lent his teammates money that was rarely paid back in full. One year during spring training, Ruth went to the racetrack on a day the game was rained out and won $9,000. At that time, players weren't paid during spring training. He gave most of his winnings to struggling teammates.

Why? Because Ruth never forgot his sad, impoverished childhood and wanted to spare others the same experience. A self-admitted incorrigible child who refused to go to school, Ruth was banished by his parents to St. Mary's Industrial School for Boys, near Baltimore. He primarily lived there, with 800 other boys, from 1904 to 1914.

Feeling deserted by his parents, Ruth looked for a role model at the school. He found one in Brother Matthias, who saw young Babe's baseball skills and encouraged him to play. Matthias told Ruth he could achieve if he kept trying.

Ruth took his message to heart. Once in professional baseball, he often gave St. Mary's a hand with fund-raising efforts and annually bought Matthias a new Cadillac.

Ruth refused to let his childhood make him bitter. Instead, he made an effort to aid children to make the world a better place.

"He was really a great person," said Ruth's daughter, Julia Ruth Stevens, in a 2003 interview. "He not only loved kids, he loved people in general. He was always trying to please his fans. He never turned down an autograph."

When he died, Ruth left much of his estate to the Babe Ruth Foundation for underprivileged children.

29

Record-Setting Receiver Jerry Rice

His Drive Launched Him Into Football Greatness

For Jerry Rice, time off doesn't mean it's time to kick back and relax. It means an opportunity to improve. Even when he was the Super Bowl's reigning Most Valuable Player.

Rice, a receiver, reached a pinnacle in pro football success in January 1989. He was in his fourth professional season with the San Francisco 49ers and playing in his first Super Bowl, against the Cincinnati Bengals.

Rice caught 11 passes for a Super Bowl record of 215 yards. He scored one touchdown as the 49ers won 20–16.

That feat required Rice to be in peak physical condition. How did he stay that way? By working out intensely in the off-season.

His workouts included running many miles a day, sprinting with a small parachute attached to his back to create resistance and challenging some of San Francisco's hardest hills by running up them.

Leading toward the 1989 season, Rice stepped it up even further in training and diet. He reported to camp 15 pounds lighter. "I felt losing weight would give me more quickness. I'm not getting any younger. There are young guys coming into camp all the time who want my job. I've got to get even better to keep my job," Rice said in Glenn Dickey's book "Sports Great Jerry Rice."

"I think this weight is better for me because I won't get fatigued late in the game. I want to eliminate mistakes, like missed blocks. When I make mistakes, it's usually because I'm fatigued," Rice said.

Rice went on to have another sensational regular season in 1989. And when the 49ers repeated as National Football League champions, Rice set Super Bowl records with 13 receptions and five touchdowns.

An Oakland Raider starting in 2001, Rice made himself arguably the greatest receiver ever and has set a new standard for the position. His former coach, Bill Walsh, called Rice "possibly the greatest football player to ever take the field, and certainly the greatest San Francisco 49er."

Through the 2003 season, he was the all-time league leader in number of receptions (1,519) and receiving yardage (22,466). Rice was named to the NFL's 75th Anniversary All-Time Team in 1994.

Getting To The Pinnacle

From the time he began playing football, Rice wanted to be the best. To get there, he mastered every football skill he could, including blocking.

"He doesn't want to be considered one-dimensional even though that one dimension is terrific," said Dickey, a veteran San Francisco sportswriter, in a 2001 interview.

Rice's off-season training was so tough, few were ever able to keep up with him. Still, he had to push himself. How? By focusing his mind only on the rewards when running the toughest hills.

"Mentally, you have to fight the quitting, and that transfers in to making the big plays, the tough plays in the game. I put myself through this type of training, so I'm in the best shape of my life during the season," Rice said in 1995.

"You don't get better unless you work hard. (Jerry is) the greatest because of his work ethic," Steve Young said in 1994 when he was the 49ers' quarterback.

Rice scored the most touchdowns in NFL history (194 at the close of 2003) and did it with class.

"I don't know who said it first, but 'when you get to the end zone, act like you've been there before . . . and (that) you'll be back.' That's Jerry Rice in a nutshell," wrote former 49er quarterback Joe Montana.

Rice knew attitude was crucial when confronting opponents, and he showed no fear on the football field. He relished running pass patterns into the middle of the field, even though he was easy prey for oncoming defensive players.

"I like the contact, and I like the courage, being able to go there, knowing you're going to get hit, and still catch the football," Rice said.

Many of Rice's touchdowns came on quick slant patterns into the middle of the field. That's because Rice was never content to just catch the ball. He wanted big gains after that. "I feel like the fun is just starting after I catch the football," he said.

His technique gave him a leading edge. "None of the other great receivers had the impact this guy does," said Hall of Fame linebacker Dick Butkus. "(Rice) controls the tempo of the game."

Rice looked at every moment on the football field as an opportunity to learn. "New guys are coming into the league all the time (who) I have to study. In a game, even if I'm a decoy receiver on a play, I run my route at top speed. I want to see how the defensive backs react to me so I'll know what I have to do when I am the receiver," he said.

Birth Of Ambition

Rice was born in Crawford, Miss., in 1962. His father was a bricklayer, and Jerry and his brothers worked with him during their summers. Waking at 6 a.m. and working straight through until 5 p.m. made a profound impression on Rice.

"When I was doing that, I thought it was the worst thing possible. But looking back, I learned I had to work hard to achieve anything in life (and) I knew I didn't want to be a bricklayer. I knew there had to be something better than that," Rice said.

It was in college at Mississippi Valley State that Rice developed his field concentration that resulted in running precise pass routes. He knew it was his strength, and he played it up.

But when Rice graduated, most NFL teams weren't impressed. Scouts were blinded by his relatively slow time. He ran the 40-yard dash in 4.6 seconds compared with the standard of 4.4 for receivers. Rice stayed confident. He was sure someone would recognize his skill.

That someone was Walsh, the 49ers' coach. He rated receivers more on their functional speed, which he felt was anywhere between 30 and 60 yards. Walsh made Rice the 16th player chosen in the 1985 draft.

Rice worked diligently on his quickness, which Montana said may be even more important to a receiver than sheer speed.

"My speed is really deceptive. A lot of defensive backs think they can check me, but this is not a track meet. It's a football game," Rice said in 1988.

Rice became a student of his playbook and a master of detail. He reviewed game tapes relentlessly, and watched like a hawk from the sidelines.

And he took pride in his uniform.

"The guys think I'm crazy. . . . They can't believe I'm taking so much time to put on my uniform," he said. "But for me, everything has to be perfect. The way I tape my shoes, the way I tuck my shirt into my pants is very important. My helmet has to be clean. My socks have to come up to just the right length."

Rice's hunger for getting things right set him apart from other athletes.

"There are certain athletes (who) want to be the best, and there are a lot of guys who are content to stay at a little lower level. They don't get near as much heat, and the expectations are not as great," Dickey said. "But a guy like Rice really wanted to be the best."

PART 4

Learning How To Be The Greatest

© Bettmann/CORBIS

It made a better person out of me. I did something wrong that cost me the race, so it made me realize that I wasn't infallible like I thought.

— WILLIE SHOEMAKER, ON HIS 1957 KENTUCKY DERBY LOSS

30

Tennis Champ
Martina Navratilova
Her Resolve To Win Helped Her
Make History

It was 1975, and 18-year-old Martina Navratilova was playing Chris Evert in the U.S. Open tennis semifinals. Evert was losing.

Then Navratilova disputed the official's call on a point that would have tied the set at 4–4. They replayed the disputed point, but Navratilova's concentration was broken. Evert went on to win the set.

The same thing happened in the second set. Frustrated, Navratilova hurled her racket to the ground. Evert won the match and went on to win the finals.

Navratilova lost a number of matches in the same fashion. She'd make a mistake and focus on it instead of her game. How was she going to be the No. 1 tennis player in the world if she couldn't learn not to dwell on her mistakes?

She decided to ask the experts. She turned to Hall of Fame pro golfer Sandra Haynie and tennis champ Billie Jean King.

"It's just understanding mistakes are gonna happen," Haynie told her. "Learn by 'em and turn 'em loose."

"I kept telling her, too, that when things go wrong, don't moan and slump and slink around. Instead, use adversity to get your gumption up and fight back," King said in "Martina: The Lives and Times of Martina Navratilova," by Adrianne Blue.

Navratilova took their advice. When she made a bad shot, she'd tell herself to ignore it and do better the next time. If she missed her opponent's shot, she'd just focus on returning the next volley with even more vigor.

"I'm very good at picking people who know what they're talking about, selecting which of their advice is most helpful for me and incorporating that into my psyche or my game," she said in an interview.

The strategy paid off. Navratilova captured the top-ranked position in the world in women's tennis in 1978, after winning the Virginia Slims championship and her first Wimbledon women's singles final.

In 1979, she again won the Wimbledon women's singles as well as a share of the women's doubles. By 2000, she held a record nine Wimbledon singles titles, as well as two French Open singles titles, three Australian Open singles titles and four U.S. Open singles titles.

By the end of 2003, Navratilova had won a total of 58 Grand Slam titles. Her 57th, the 2003 Australian Open win in mixed doubles, made her the oldest Grand Slam champion in tennis history. Her 1987 victories in the U.S. Open singles, women's doubles and mixed doubles made her the first triple-crown champion at the U.S. Open since 1970.

Her 158th title win in Chicago in 1992 gave her the most championships of any player in tennis history, male or female. She continued to hold that record at the end of 2003 with 167 singles tournament wins. In 2000, Navratilova was inducted into the International Tennis Hall of Fame.

To get there, though, Navratilova worked hard. In addition to putting in countless hours of practice, she never feared to ask others to critique her game.

Take her try for a record ninth Wimbledon singles title in 1990. Navratilova was seeking to break the 52-year-old record of eight titles, which she shared with Helen Wills Moody. Navratilova was coming off a loss in Florida to a newcomer, Gabriela Sabatini. Navratilova had played poorly.

"My technique was so bad that I had to stop and think about every shot," she said.

Labor Of Love

To prepare for Wimbledon, Navratilova analyzed her shots. She looked at how she stepped into her swing. But she couldn't figure out exactly what she was doing wrong.

Navratilova realized that she'd need some tough coaching. So she called King and asked her to help.

King did and assessed Navratilova's game. While the two talked, Navratilova realized she'd become burned out and needed to rediscover her pure love for the game.

"To be successful in anything, you have to love what you're doing," she said.

She also studied other players. As soon as she learned something new, she'd incorporate it into her own game.

"I would learn a new stroke and use it later the same day or the next day in a match. Most people take months and months to be able to do that," she said.

Navratilova succeeded in capturing her ninth Wimbledon singles title, a record that still stands.

Aiming High

Winning Wimbledon had been a dream for her from early childhood. At 4½, Martina saw people playing tennis and wanted to learn. She started hitting balls against a wall with an old racket at her home in Revnice, Czechoslovakia. She'd hit the balls for hours, trying to aim them higher, then lower.

As she grew a little older, her stepfather started hitting balls to her and encouraged her to pretend she was playing at Wimbledon. That way, she'd always play her best, he figured.

That's exactly what she tried to do. Every time she stepped on a court, Navratilova urged herself to fire nothing but her best shots. She visualized beating her opponent.

She played in her first tournament at 8 years old.

Then she saw her first Wimbledon match on television. "I remember watching Billie Jean win; that was in 1966. I thought I could do it one day," Navratilova said.

She was determined to reach her goal. She practiced harder than ever to hone her game. She listened closely to her coaches' advice. She drilled herself over and over.

By the time she was 16, she was a top player in the Czech Tennis Federation. She won the 1972 Czech national singles championship and began traveling to the U.S. for tournaments in 1973.

The Communist-controlled Czech Tennis Federation constrained her ability to compete worldwide, though. To be the best, she needed to compete more. She turned the problem over in her head. Could she persuade the federation to allow her to travel more?

She couldn't. But she could figure out a way to help herself. At 18, the night before her 1975 U.S. Open semifinal match against Evert, Navratilova walked into a U.S. Immigration and Naturalization Service office and asked for asylum.

"I knew I wanted to play tennis, and to do that I knew I had to leave the country," she said.

It wasn't easy. She faced her fear, though, and took the step she knew would give her the chances she longed for.

"I feared what would happen to my family. Would I ever be able to see them again? Would I ever be able to come back to Czechoslovakia? And would they ever be able to leave the country?" she recalled. "But at 18 or 19, you just kind of believe everything will work out."

She maintained that positive attitude throughout her career. In fact, she says, it's key to any success.

"You have to keep a positive attitude," she said. "You have to remember you have no control over anything but your attitude."

31

Jockey Willie Shoemaker

Relentless Determination
Helped Put Him In The Lead

Willie Shoemaker was riding high. After winning the 1955 Kentucky Derby, he'd claimed repeated victories to become the nation's premier jockey by the end of 1956.

So when the gates opened for the 1957 Kentucky Derby, Shoemaker figured he'd win as handily as the other times.

But there was one problem. He hadn't raced on the track, Churchill Downs, in a year, and had forgotten about its unique configuration.

As Shoemaker's horse, "Gallant Man," passed the 16th pole in the home stretch, the jockey raised his arms to signify victory. But the celebration was premature: the finish line was 1/16 of a mile away. Another horse, "Iron Liege," nosed past his and won.

Shoemaker (1931–2003) realized his gaffe. From then on until he retired in 1990, he took the time to become familiar with every track before racing on it.

He was also humbled. "It made a better person out of me," he said. "I did something wrong that cost me the race, so it made me realize that I wasn't infallible like I thought."

That willingness to learn from his mistakes helped Shoemaker get to the top. During his 41-year career, he rode more mounts (40,350) than anyone in racing history. Until December 1999, he'd won the most races (8,813) of any jockey in racing. His Triple Crown wins consisted of four Kentucky Derbys, five Belmont Stakes and two Preakness Stakes. Named to the National Horse Racing Hall of

Fame in 1958, he was the first jockey whose mounts won more than $100 million.

Hanging Tough

Shoemaker had always hung tough — an essential skill when a petite jockey is riding 1,000-pound horses at up to 40 miles per hour.

The young Shoemaker, born prematurely at about 2½ pounds, grew up poor in Fabens, Texas. His father was a tenant farmer. The oven provided the heat for the house. His parents were divorced when he was 3, and he lived with his mother and other relatives.

At 10, he moved to El Monte, Calif. In high school, bigger and stronger boys picked on the 4-foot-11, 90-pound Shoemaker.

He refused to take their attacks lying down. To defend himself, he joined the school's wrestling and boxing teams to learn how to fight back.

He worked hard in the gym, sparring over and over with opponents. He also lifted weights daily to become stronger in the arms and legs.

His commitment paid off. He boxed in some 30 matches in high school and excelled in the 95- to 105-pound category. He got so good that he won the Los Angeles Golden Gloves tournament.

Meanwhile, a female friend suggested that because of his small build he should ride horses for a living. She introduced him to her boyfriend, a jockey, who took Shoemaker to a La Puente, Calif., ranch that trained thoroughbreds.

Shoemaker immediately fell in love with the horses. He decided his future lay with them, so he quit high school and headed straight for the ranch. He spent two years there, learning how to take care of and ride horses.

He made the most of the experience, working nearly around the clock. He groomed and walked the horses. He carted in hay from fields to feed them. He cleaned out stalls, and harrowed and watered the track. He questioned trainers and other experts about the horses and their behavior. He watched closely as the trainers broke in yearlings.

All along, Shoemaker wanted to race. But he didn't want to become just any jockey. He saw himself being the best. So he took his time, making sure he mastered the skills he knew he'd need.

"I knew I had to work hard to impress on people that I was serious about what I wanted to be," he said. "I figured if I worked hard and showed an interest, they would show an interest in me."

He sought out current and former jockeys to ask their advice. One ex-jockey showed him how to cross the reins and sit on a horse properly. Another showed him how to maintain balance while the horse ran. After a while, Shoemaker was comfortable in the saddle.

Shoemaker absorbed these tips and practiced at the track during nearly every moment of down time he had. Gradually, he gained a strong feel for the animals by learning, for example, how to communicate with them.

Jockey-horse communication is critical. Shoemaker learned how to "talk" to the animal and make a timid horse bolder or quiet a high-strung horse using rein position and leg movements.

He also worked on acting quickly when he made an observation. He had to know when to hold a horse back, cut to the outside, go to the rail or take advantage of an opening in front of him. He'd drill himself mentally while riding, checking and rechecking his horse's response to different movements.

"I learned right off that a rider couldn't ride any faster than a horse could run, but I knew there were tricks and there was an ability that made one rider different than other riders," he wrote in his autobiography, "Shoemaker: America's Greatest Jockey." "A rider with good hands sends a message to his horse through the reins. A horse knows kind hands from rough, insensitive hands."

Learning From The Best

In 1948, Shoemaker approached Hurst Philpot, a horse trainer at a track near San Francisco, for a job as a jockey. Philpot watched Shoemaker gallop some of his good horses and wasn't impressed. He didn't think Shoemaker had what it took to be successful in real races, so he hired him to exercise horses.

Shoemaker refused to let someone else's attitude get in his way and ignored Philpot's pronouncement. At the same time, he knew he needed to learn more before he could race horses for a living.

So Shoemaker regularly watched one of Philpot's jockeys, Johnny Adams, in action. Shoemaker learned from Adams how to pace and rate a horse, or determine what the horse likes and dislikes, such as whipping. He also realized how much a jockey could do with his hands.

When he'd learned all he could from Adams, Shoemaker quit Philpot and got a job with George Reeves, a trainer at another local track. Reeves trained fewer horses than Philpot and was able to pay more attention to Shoemaker.

He made sure that he kept practicing so he'd be ready if an opportunity arose. It did — Reeves noticed Shoemaker's racing skills and introduced him to an agent, who arranged for Shoemaker to work at Golden Gate Fields, a track near Oakland. Shoemaker galloped horses at Golden Gate Fields and cleaned out stalls.

Shoemaker quickly gained the respect of horse owners, trainers and fellow jockeys. Yet he wasn't content. He still wanted to improve.

He looked for another expert to learn from and decided on Eddie Arcaro, then one of the world's best jockeys. Shoemaker would watch as many of Arcaro's races as he could, then zero in on his techniques. He memorized the way Arcaro sat, brought a horse out of the gate, ran a horse.

Later, Shoemaker would try to repeat what he'd seen Arcaro do. Once he'd mastered a move, he'd try to learn another.

After years of trying to gain attention, Shoemaker began racing at Golden Gate Fields in March 1949 and soon earned his first victory. By year's end, he had 219 wins, a mark second to only one other jockey in the country. He was No. 1 in 1950, claiming 388 victories that year.

Shoemaker later became the oldest jockey to win a Kentucky Derby when, at age 54, he rode "Ferdinand" to one last Run-for-the-Roses victory in 1986.

His determination didn't stop at the racetrack. For six years after a 1991 car accident left him paralyzed below the neck, Shoemaker continued training horses from a wheelchair.

32

Heavyweight Boxer
Joe Louis

Unwavering Discipline Made
Him Longest-Reigning Champ

Joe Louis was knocked down seven times in just two rounds in his first amateur fight. The trouncing kept him away from boxing for six months.

But boxing was Louis' passion. He was determined to make it as a fighter. He decided he needed to learn from the people who'd bested him in the ring.

Louis studied other fighters, watching their footwork and hitting styles. He figured out what he could adapt. He memorized different punches, training his mind as rigorously as his body.

The result? Five years later, Louis (1914–81) won the world heavyweight title. He knocked out James J. Braddock in 1937 and held the title until 1949, when he retired undefeated as champ. No other boxer has held the top title as long. Louis defended his crown 25 times; 20 of those wins came by knockout.

Strict Guidelines

Louis' career took off after he turned pro in 1934 and asked John Roxborough to manage him. Roxborough set down stiff rules: a strict diet, rigorous training and no easy fights. But the guidelines went beyond that. Nightclubs were out. To fight well, Louis had to live clean.

Sportswriters chalked up Louis' prowess to his clean living, Bible reading and gentlemanly ways. He didn't smoke or drink. While training, he once ordered the camp bar closed because he said he didn't want any "drunks slobbering around," according to Anthony O. Edmonds in "Joe Louis."

Roxborough enlisted Jack Blackburn to train Louis. Blackburn had Louis wake up each day at 6 a.m. and run twice around a city park — six miles in all. Louis then went back to sleep until 11 a.m., when he woke for breakfast.

For most of the afternoon, Louis was in the gym. During the first week of training, Blackburn didn't let him near the ring. Blackburn steadied a heavy bag as Louis punched away.

With each blow, Blackburn felt the heaviness growing in Louis' punches. But power itself doesn't win titles. Louis' hands, however strong, were too slow. To develop speed, Louis started sparring with lighter, quicker boxers. He had to speed his own pace to match theirs. Louis' resulting mix of power and agility devastated opponents.

"Through diligent study and hard training, (Louis) rose to the position of a sophisticated product, a boxing machine," Edmonds wrote.

Biographer John G. van Deusen said, "Steady, hard work and careful preparation made Louis the greatest fighting machine since (Jack) Dempsey."

Louis also learned mental discipline from Blackburn. As a black fighter in a polarized society, Louis was up against more than tough opponents. In "Champion: Joe Louis, Black Hero in White America," author Chris Mead says Blackburn warned Louis he'd never win the title by merely outscoring white opponents.

"You gotta knock 'em out to get anywhere," Blackburn told Louis. "You gotta knock 'em out and keep knocking 'em out."

Louis had already come a long way. He was born Joe Louis Barrow in 1914. He dropped Barrow early on after a starting bell rang before he could finish giving his full name to the ring announcer.

Years Of Training

A native of Lafayette, Ala., Louis grew up poor. When Joe was only 2, his father was hospitalized for mental illness, leaving Joe's mother to care for eight children in a run-down house.

Joe's mother remarried in 1924, and the family moved to Detroit.

While at a trade school, Louis discovered boxing. The burly youngster immediately recognized that it was something he did well. Yet he knew he'd need more training if he wanted to excel. He worked at a truck factory all day and trained at night and on the weekends.

After years of training, Louis became a professional boxer in 1934. In his first year, he fought regularly against tough opponents — beating them all. He focused all his energy on searching out their weak spots in the ring, then hitting them there as hard and as often as he could.

On his reputation as a tough fighter, Louis soon lined up a bout in New York City. That alone was a triumph for a black boxer in the mid-1930s. In his first bout in the Big Apple, Louis destroyed former heavyweight champ Primo Carnera.

By 1937, Louis was ready for his first title fight. He prepared at an estate on Lake Michigan in Wisconsin. He was more serious than ever, training almost all his waking hours.

"There was little of the fooling around that had marked previous camps," wrote Richard Bak, author of "Joe Louis: The Great Black Hope."

Louis kept a strict schedule, rising at 5 a.m. and running 10 miles. Then it was back to bed until a breakfast of prunes, orange juice, and liver or lamb chops at 10 a.m.

For dinner, Louis ate chicken, fish and vegetables. Sweets, which he loved, had no place in the future champ's diet. When Louis was given a huge cake for his 23rd birthday, his discipline was tested. He stayed focused, restricting himself to one small slice. He still needed to lose 10 pounds to get into his best fighting shape.

All his preparation worked. Louis knocked out Braddock, the champ, in the eighth round to win the title.

Winning Attitude

Louis' road to the title had some bumps. Before beating Braddock, he lost to German fighter Max Schmeling in 1936. Even after gaining the crown, Louis said he wouldn't answer to the title of champ until he beat Schmeling in a rematch.

The rematch came in 1938. Louis didn't repeat the mistakes he made before the first fight. Press attention and his new wife had distracted Louis the first time around. Trainer Blackburn said he played too much golf back then.

So Louis trained harder than ever for the second Schmeling fight. He didn't spend too much time with reporters. With Blackburn he watched films of the first bout, carefully noting the errors he'd made. Louis was so focused that his "mental attitude is the best I've ever known him to attain," manager Roxborough said.

For the first time in years, Louis didn't bring his golf clubs to camp.

The dedication paid off. Louis knocked out Schmeling in the first round as the cheers of the crowd rang in Yankee Stadium.

Louis defended the heavyweight title in 25 bouts, more times than any other champion. His willingness to take on any challenger defined his greatness. A lesser boxer would've lost sometime in that busy schedule, but Louis looked at his fights as good conditioning — the regular bouts kept him in shape.

Louis retired undefeated as champ in 1949. Twice he tried comebacks, but never regained the title. He retired for good in 1951, having lost only three times in 71 pro fights.

33

Swimming Champ
Mark Spitz

Drive For Excellence Made Him
The Best

Mark Spitz achieved his greatest triumph because he refused to dwell on his biggest disappointment: his performance in the 1968 Olympics.

Instead, the then-18-year-old Spitz decided to learn from the experience.

Many athletes would have been happy with the four medals (two gold, a silver and a bronze) that Spitz won that year in Mexico City. But not Spitz.

He'd lost in two individual events, the 100- and 200-meter butterfly, even though he held the respective world records. His gold medals were as part of relay teams. After the games, Spitz carefully analyzed what went wrong.

He realized that he'd never swum the three individual events he was entered in at the same competition before. He'd allowed his disappointment in losing an event to carry over to the next one.

"I wasn't capable of going from one event to another, leaving everything that happened the day before behind and treating each individual day as its own entity," Spitz, said in a 2001 interview.

"You cannot carry what did or did not happen from one day to the next, especially if it's negative, into something that's supposed to be a positive experience for the next day."

Also, during the Olympics training camp Doug Russell beat him in the 100-meter butterfly. "All that did was instill a lot of positive thinking in his mind and a lot of negative thinking in mine," Spitz said. Russell went on to win the gold medal in the event.

During the next four years leading up to the 1972 Olympics, Spitz spent his time correcting his mistakes. He practiced by getting himself used to swimming all the events (now adding the 200-meter freestyle) at the same competitions. He prepared himself mentally to go from event to event, telling himself to ignore his prior performance and focus on the next. To keep his opponents from gaining too much confidence, he tried to beat them soundly in competitions.

He won and won and won. At the 1972 Olympic Games, held in Munich, Germany, Spitz became the first man to win seven gold medals in one Olympics, and set seven world records in the process. Four of his gold medals were in individual events (100- and 200-meter freestyle and butterfly).

"To me, the value of being in the Olympic games taught me that no matter how successful you think you might be, you become actually more successful after you've failed miserably," Spitz said.

"Mark's unparalleled feat at the 1972 Munich Olympics (is) regarded by many as the greatest Olympic performance in any sport, ever," wrote Phillip Whitten in 1995 in *Swimming World Magazine*.

Spitz's nine gold medals are the most ever for a swimmer in Olympic history, and they tie him with four others for the most gold medals in the summer Olympics. In 1977, he was inducted into the International Swimming Hall of Fame as an Honor Swimmer. *Swimming World Magazine* and the Swimming Hall of Fame named Spitz the Male Swimmer of the Century.

Spitz's pursuit of perfection resulted in his setting 17 world records in the last 20 events of his career. In all, Spitz set 26 world records.

"The value of sport to me is that experience is the most valuable thing that you've got, and with that, you can use that tool as a springboard to do better," he said.

It's All Relative

When training, Spitz didn't just focus on working out hard — he directed himself to work out fast.

"There's a major difference, because a lot of us have the impression we work out hard, but that doesn't have any relativity," Spitz said. "If you're fast, it's a relationship to time, or distance, or score. You know what it takes to win because there are benchmarks within your area of expertise. Even in the business world your performance is based on a known value."

Spitz believes there's a fine line between preparation and participation. "Too many people in life spend too much time keeping score, so it's impossible for them to play the game," he said. While it's important to master details, you shouldn't lose sight of the big picture, he says.

"Just get off your behind and do it. It doesn't matter if you didn't do it right, because not doing it at all is definitely not doing it right."

Spitz understands the importance of being in control of one's own destiny. When he was just 13, he decided he was tired of losing swimming meets to two other boys.

"I remember going up to my coach and saying 'How come Mike and Mitch keep beating me?' and the guy said 'That's OK, Mark, your times are improving,'" Spitz recalled. "I walked away very discouraged saying 'OK, my times are improving, but theirs are getting faster.'"

"I'm swimming and getting my brains beat out by these two guys and I realize their coach has got a lot of other great swimmers, and that even though I'm the best swimmer on my team, maybe I can't go any further. I've maxed out this opportunity."

To improve his speed, Spitz figured he'd better train with those who could beat him in the water. Spitz went to his father and told him he wanted to switch coaches from his own to George Haines, who coached the boys who were beating him.

Spitz's father moved the family from Walnut Creek (in Northern California) 85 miles to Santa Clara, Calif., so Spitz could swim under Haines' guidance and with other future Olympians at the Santa Clara Swim Club.

From 14 to 18, Spitz swam under the instruction of Haines, who also coached him in the 1968 Olympics. Haines is a seven-time Olympic swimming coach and was named by both *Swimming World Magazine* and the Swimming Hall of Fame as coach of the century.

He literally soaked up everything Haines told him to expand his skills.

"When you told Mark something, when you corrected something in his stroke, you never had to remind him again," Haines said.

Attitude And Effort

Spitz's talent is as much a result of attitude as physical effort, say those who know him.

"Mark is one of these people who just can't conceive of the possibility that he will lose in anything. He will do whatever it takes legitimately to beat you," said Whitten, who also swam under Haines and is now editor in chief of *Swimming World Magazine*.

Spitz became a successful investment consultant to financial consortiums and a real estate developer. His real estate company, Spitz-Selco, builds upper-end homes, complete with an original "Mark Spitz" pool, in the Los Angeles area.

While a competitive spirit has helped him in the business world, Spitz knows that isn't all he needs. Without integrity, he says, customers won't trust you. He makes every effort to live up to everything he says he'll do.

"One of the great things about Mark is he's a tremendously loyal friend," said Whitten, a longtime friend of Spitz. "Mark is scrupulously honest and a man of his word."

A sought-after public speaker, Spitz says many of the lessons he learned as an athlete have served him well in the business world.

"In sports or business, you need patience," he said. "You have to have a blueprint and a plan to follow that's based on experts that are far more capable than you are.

"It's like with my coaches. I went to the great coaches and listened to them and their tutelage. Today, if I have a problem I go to people (who) are experts in their field, and I attach myself to them."

34

Basketball Coach
John Wooden
Careful Analysis Helped Him
Scale The Pyramid Of Success

In 1965, John Wooden, basketball coach at the University of California, Los Angeles, won his second straight NCAA championship. But he wasn't about to coast on the achievement.

Instead, Wooden looked to the future. He'd been using the same high-post offense since he'd started coaching more than 30 years earlier, but now he decided change was necessary. And he was willing to learn something entirely new in order to bring it about.

The reason? The nation's most dominating high school player, center Lew Alcindor (later known as Kareem Abdul-Jabbar), was coming to UCLA. Wooden wanted to install a single low-post offense because he knew it would help develop Alcindor's considerable skills while giving the team the best chance to win. Wooden had never used the single low post before, and for the next year and a half he worked hard at learning its intricacies.

"I spent a great deal of time talking to coaches whom I respected about the low-post offense. I watched hours of film on it," Wooden said in a 2000 interview.

The results? Three more NCAA championships (1967–69) with Alcindor leading the way. Five more championships followed after Alcindor graduated, with both high- and low-post offenses.

Wooden won a record total of 10 national basketball championships, including seven in a row from 1967 to 1973. He holds the longest winning streak in NCAA history at 88 games in a row.

"Be open-minded," Wooden said. "There is no progress without change."

Court Analysis

"(Wooden's) willingness to listen to the ideas of others and his lack of ego allowed him to change and keep up with the ever-changing game," wrote Denny Crum, a former Wooden assistant and currently head basketball coach at the University of Louisville.

During his first 12 seasons of coaching at UCLA, Wooden had teams that qualified for the tournament and that he felt could have won championships but didn't. So after the 1960 season, Wooden decided to examine everything he was doing as a coach.

He went over plays, looked at his extensive daily notes, watched game films and asked his assistants what they remembered. Wooden determined he'd been working his players too hard in practices and that they were worn out by the time of the NCAA tournament.

Wooden introduced a rotation system into his intense, full-speed practices. This gave his starting five players more rest. It also improved teamwork by giving the top reserves more time with the starters. The team looked and felt better — but still won no championships.

With his 1963 and 1964 teams, Wooden saw that he had the necessary quickness in his personnel to force turnovers, so he installed a full-court zone press to harass opponents.

Although his players fell short in 1963, by 1964 their play was solid. The 1964 team, with no starter taller than 6-foot-5, was the culmination of Wooden's efforts and won his first NCAA title.

Wooden wrote in his 1997 book "Wooden" that he won championships because he correctly "analyzed players, (got) them to fill roles as part of a team, paid attention to fundamentals and details, and worked well with others."

To keep his players motivated to do their best, Wooden let them know he cared about them as people rather than just as players.

While his achievements pushed him to living-legend status, "being around him you would have never known it," said Jamaal

Wilkes, a two-time All-American at UCLA in 1972 and 1973. "Consideration for others was really very important to him."

It is also important to remain humble, Wooden believes.

"I felt just as successful a coach in all the years I didn't win championships," Wooden said. "Success is peace of mind, which is a direct result of self-satisfaction in knowing you did your best to become the best you are capable of becoming."

In fact, that definition of success is the apex of his famed "Pyramid of Success" diagram.

Wooden taught his players the Pyramid of Success, consisting of five tiers and 15 blocks. The blocks emphasize such virtues as cooperation, loyalty and building confidence through preparation.

"To really work hard at something you must enjoy it," Wooden wrote of the cornerstones of the pyramid — industriousness and enthusiasm.

Implementing each block is crucial, Wooden says, in preparation for achieving "competitive greatness," which he defines as "being at your best when your best is needed and is positioned just under the apex of success."

To stay on top of his job, Wooden studied other successful coaches. He analyzed the way the great Notre Dame football coach Frank Leahy organized practices.

It's In The Planning

Wooden believed the foundation of winning was developed during practice, and he spent up to two hours daily planning each one.

"I've always considered a coach to be a teacher," Wooden wrote in his book "They Call Me Coach."

At practice, Wooden taught fundamentals by repetition. Rather than using lengthy playbooks or chalkboard diagrams, Wooden found his team learned best "verbally, bit by bit, right there on the court. The best teacher is repetition, day after day," he said.

Wooden believes a coach's primary job is to prepare players to play. "I've used the statement a lot that 'Failure to prepare is preparing to fail,'" Wooden said.

No coach can win consistently without talented players, Wooden says. He made sure his reputation was sterling so that athletes would want to play for him. Yet Wooden refused to talk players into coming to UCLA.

"I wanted them to want to come to UCLA," Wooden said. "I would never promise a player that he would play. Playing time had to be earned. More than anything else in recruiting, you have to be completely honest."

Players appreciated it. "I felt I'd get a fair shake and that he'd be a good influence on me," Wilkes said.

Wooden offered scholarships only to players who were good students and possessed good moral character.

"Academic progress should always come first," Wooden told his players (most of whom graduated), but "basketball should take precedence over good times."

Wooden knew firsthand the distractions that athletes can face. He was an outstanding student at Purdue University and a three-time All-American basketball player. In 1932, Wooden was College Player of the Year and won the Big Ten medal for scholarship and athletics.

He'd wanted to do his best from the start. Wooden wrote of his "driving desire to be the best-conditioned player in basketball." As a coach, he made sure no team was better conditioned than his.

He taught players his pyramid virtues of mental and physical discipline on and off the court. He insisted they be well groomed and in top physical condition. "There is no replacement for sound fundamentals and strict discipline," Wooden wrote.

He also made sure he was in good physical and mental shape. "A coach (must) maintain mental and emotional balance at all times if he or she is to teach well and make productive decisions," Wooden wrote.

"Coach taught us self-discipline and was always his own best example," Abdul-Jabbar said in "Wooden."

Wooden, a devout Christian, tried to stand up for what he thought was right. In 1946, as head coach at Indiana State, he refused an invitation to the National Association of Intercollegiate Athletics (NAIA) basketball tournament because it wouldn't allow his only black player, a little-used reserve, to participate. "Coach Wooden doesn't see color," said Curtis Rowe, a black player at UCLA, in 1970.

Wooden's wisdom still influences players.

"I still have his pyramid on my desk," Wilkes said.

35

Runner Roger Bannister

He Broke The Four-Minute Mile, Proving There Are No Limits

Roger Bannister's first step in breaking the four-minute-mile barrier was shattering a mental hurdle.

Prior to May 6, 1954, most of the world thought that running a mile in less than four minutes was impossible.

After all, runners had failed for decades to seize what had become the sport's Holy Grail. The four-minute mile was widely seen as an obstacle — both physical and psychological — that exceeded human limits.

But not by Bannister, an athlete and medical student at Oxford University. He wondered whether the biggest obstacle runners faced might not be their own beliefs.

"There was no rational reason why somebody can run a 4:01.4 mile (the nine-year record Bannister would break) and with slightly better conditions or better training or even pacing, not do it in 3:59.4. It doesn't stand to reason, does it?" Bannister said in a 1998 interview.

Bannister became fascinated by the challenge of proving the limits were self-imposed.

"The four-minute mile had become like an Everest — a challenge to the human spirit," he wrote in his book "The Four Minute Mile," published in 1956. "It was a barrier that seemed to defy attempts to break it — an irksome reminder that man's striving might be in vain."

He studied the problem as he would any experiment — scientifically. That "increased my understanding of the common sense of it," Bannister said.

He read up on the physiology of breaking the barrier and confirmed for himself that while it could exhaust his physical endurance, it was possible.

Bannister "demystified the psychological barrier (that had tripped up other runners) by analyzing it logically," said Jim Dunaway, senior editor of *Track & Field News* and author of "The Four Minute Mile: 1954–1967." Breaking the four-minute barrier "was the biggest thunderclap in track and field history, and for many people still is." Indeed, by the end of 1955, there had been four other sub-four-minute-mile races.

But as Bannister envisioned his race, he unwittingly began setting limitations for himself, just as the runners before him had. He began to believe that conditions at the track would have to be ideal for him to break the record. But at least he had a possible framework.

"I had run time trials which indicated I should be able to do it. I was among a bunch of three or four runners in the world for whom it was possible."

Bannister began training for the perfect race. His pace would have to be consistent. He couldn't waste energy jostling other runners for position.

Ideally, he'd run four quarter-miles in less than one minute each. At the end of the last leg, he'd sprint to make the best use of oxygen. Bannister's goal: To use his last bit of energy as he hit the tape.

He prepared for the record assault through the winter of 1953–54. As he would the day of the race, he ran in short, spirited bouts. In fact, he ran no more than 30 minutes a day.

"I trained to exhaustion in the half hour," he recalled. "As the length of the race was only four minutes, that was what I needed."

He cross-trained to build endurance. To strengthen the muscles in the back of his legs, he'd often run uphill and downhill on grass. He also did interval work, breaking up his 60-second, quarter-mile bursts with light jogging.

About one month before the race, he went hiking for several days to clear his head and focus his concentration. Five days before the attempt, he stopped training.

The day of the race, he traveled from London to Oxford. Blustery winds were blowing across the Iffley Road track.

Having convinced himself that he needed perfect weather to break the four-minute barrier, Bannister considered throwing in the towel. But trainer Franz Stampfl stepped in.

"I think he helped fill me with the confidence that I ought to attempt it, even though the weather was less than ideal," Bannister said. "If I didn't, I might not get another chance. It was a matter of believing that logic."

He wrote, "(I had) reached my peak physically and psychologically. There would never be another day like it. I think you have to take chances. You've got to balance the pros and the cons, and then you have to make a decision."

He wavered until five minutes before the race. Running mates Chris Brasher and Chris Chataway both agreed to be pace setters. They "had their part to play by running the right race, which they did," Bannister said.

Stoked by the importance of the event, Brasher posted a record-setting half-mile pace that Chataway took over in the third lap. Some 300 yards from the tape, Bannister passed Chataway and poured it on.

He "had to refuse to give in to crushing fatigue as well as oxygen debt, and not buckle under lactic-acid overload," said Amby Burfoot, the editor of *Runner's World* magazine. "He had to find another gear just as he was approaching the brink of collapse."

"My body had long since exhausted all its energy," Bannister recalled of his final sprint. "But I went on running just the same. The physical overdraft came only from great will power."

Bannister lunged forward into the tape, fell exhausted into outstretched arms and awaited confirmation that he had cleared the barrier. "I knew I had done it, even before I heard the time, of 3:59.4," Bannister said.

The runner, who went on to become a medical doctor in Oxford and London, has this advice about tackling challenge: "Analyze it strategically. Work out what the various aspects of that success will be. Make sure it's a target within your compass. Make sure it is best suited for your personality. If the answers to all those things are positive, then you have to go for it."

PART 5

Without Risk, There Is No Success

© NewSport/CORBIS

Only by acknowledging the possibility of defeat can you fully experience the joy of competition. Winning is important to me, but what brings me real joy is being fully engaged in whatever I'm doing.

— PHIL JACKSON

36

Baseball Player
Jackie Robinson
Dedication Helped Him
Become A Legend

There seemed no light at the end of the tunnel for infielder Jackie Robinson early in the 1947 baseball season.

He was in his rookie year as modern baseball's first major-league black player, and he'd been prepared for the vicious racial slurs he was receiving from opposing players and spectators. He'd been prepared to be rejected by some of his teammates.

What he wasn't ready for was a deep batting slump. No matter how well Robinson handled race baiting, integration in baseball would fail unless he produced as a ballplayer.

Almost two years earlier, Robinson (1919–72) and Brooklyn Dodger President Branch Rickey agreed that Robinson wouldn't answer racial taunts by fighting. Fighting could set off race riots in the stadium, and those opposing integration would use that to justify excluding blacks from playing in the major leagues.

To win the battle for integration and acceptance, Rickey told Robinson, "Our weapons will be base hits and stolen bases and swallowed pride."

With the Dodgers as hosts for the Philadelphia Phillies for a three-game series early in the 1947 season, Robinson was subjected to the worst kind of racial slurs from Phillie players, led by their manager, Ben Chapman. But Robinson restrained himself, kept quiet and let his playing do the talking.

In the eighth inning of the first game, Robinson finally tuned out the name-calling and gave his complete focus to his play.

He singled, ending a one-for-20 batting slump. A master base runner who'd learned from the best, he stole second base, went to third when the throw went into center field, and scored the winning run on a single.

By the third game of the series, the race baiting intensified. Finally Dodger infielder Eddie Stanky yelled to the Phillies' dugout, "Listen, you yellow-bellied cowards, why don't you yell at somebody who can answer back?"

Robinson's intense, daring play throughout the season won him renown as the first National League Rookie of the Year in 1947 and helped the Dodgers win the league pennant that year. He also gained peace of mind.

"I had learned how to exercise self-control — to answer insults, violence and injustice with silence — and I had learned how to earn the respect of my teammates," Robinson wrote in "I Never Had It Made: An Autobiography."

Robinson, who began his major-league career at the baseball-advanced age of 28, played 10 seasons with the Dodgers, compiling a lifetime batting average of .311. He helped lead the Dodgers to six National League pennants and one world championship. He was elected to the Baseball Hall of Fame in 1962. Robinson was selected as a second baseman on Major League Baseball's All-Century Team in 1999.

"(Robinson) was a great competitor who could do it all. He was a great player, a manager's dream. . . . If I had to go to war, I'd want him on my side," said Hall of Fame manager Leo Durocher, who managed Robinson in 1948.

Major Impact

Yet Robinson's impact off the field was even larger than his success on it. "He underwent the trauma and the humiliation and the loneliness which comes with being a pilgrim walking the lonesome byways toward the high road of freedom," said the Rev. Martin Luther King Jr. in 1962.

In 1997, to honor Robinson's memory on the 50th anniversary of his breaking baseball's color barrier, Major League Baseball took the unprecedented step of retiring Robinson's number, 42, from every team. Players wearing 42 then, though, could keep it until retirement.

"Jack said that a life is not important except for the impact it has on the lives of others," said Rachel Robinson, Jackie's widow, in an interview. "He really lived by that. He never looked for self-aggrandizement."

Robinson credited his success to the love and support of his wife. His values were guided by a strong religious faith. He believed his skills were God-given and aided by continual practice.

"Jack's spirituality and his deep devotion to his religion had a lot to do with the way he behaved and performed," Rachel Robinson said. "He prayed a lot, and he believed that God would take care of him if he did his part."

Robinson demanded the best from himself and took action when he didn't achieve it. For example, after an extensive off-season on the banquet circuit, Robinson was 25 pounds overweight by the start of spring training in 1948. His poor conditioning led to a slow start for him, and the Dodgers managed only a third-place finish.

Although Robinson's final numbers weren't bad in 1948 (a .296 batting average with 85 runs batted in), "In my heart I was miserable. I knew that I should have done better — much better. I made myself a solemn vow to redeem myself and the Dodgers in 1949," Robinson said in "Jackie Robinson: A Biography" by Arnold Rampersad.

Robinson, who didn't smoke or drink, put himself on a tough conditioning regimen, exercising several hours every day. He reported to spring training in 1949 slimmed down and in shape.

To improve his hitting, the right-handed Robinson learned something new — hitting the ball to right field. He hit the ball relentlessly in practice that spring to develop the needed split-second timing.

His efforts paid off as Robinson won the National League batting crown with a .342 average. He knocked in 124 runs while leading the league in stolen bases and the Dodgers to the pennant. In 1949, Robinson was named the league's Most Valuable Player.

Leading By Example

"He'd put on his game face and was all business," said former Dodger outfielder Duke Snider, a teammate of Robinson's and a fellow member of the Hall of Fame. "He showed his intensity by his example on the field."

According to his wife, Robinson was a thinking player who studied opposing pitchers to learn their strengths and weaknesses before he faced them.

His baseball achievements gave him a platform, and Robinson used it to speak out and write forcefully on civil rights during and after his playing career. When a prominent sportswriter told Robinson that he was offending other sportswriters and might cost himself awards they voted on, Robinson remained undeterred.

"If I had a room jammed with trophies, awards and citations," Robinson wrote, "and a child of mine came to me into that room and asked what I had done in defense of black people and decent whites fighting for freedom — and I had to tell that child I had kept quiet, that I had been timid, I would have to mark myself a total failure in the whole business of living."

Nine days before his death in 1972, Robinson threw out the first ball for the second game of the World Series in Cincinnati. He was suffering from diabetes and nearly blind, but his spirit was still strong. Major-league teams still hadn't hired a black manager, and Robinson reminded everyone of that while accepting a plaque in his honor.

"I'm going to be tremendously more pleased and more proud when I look at that third-base coaching line one day and see a black face managing in baseball," Robinson told the crowd.

Among baseball players, "only Jackie Robinson insisted, day in and day out, on challenging America on the matter of race and justice," biographer Rampersad wrote.

"I learned a long time ago that a person must be true to himself if he is to succeed," Robinson wrote in a letter to a friend in the mid-1950s. "He must be willing to stand by his principles."

37

Tennis Player
Althea Gibson
She Made Her Hits Count

A fire burned deep in Althea Gibson.

"I always wanted to be somebody. It's why I took to tennis right away and kept working at it," said Gibson, who died in September 2003 at age 76. "I've worshipped (legendary boxer and friend) Sugar Ray Robinson. It wasn't just because he was a wonderful fellow, and good to me when there was no special reason for him to be; it was because he was somebody, and I was determined that I was going to be somebody, too."

Raised in wretched poverty in New York City's Harlem, Gibson broke the color barrier in the all-white, upscale, country-club world of the U.S. Lawn Tennis Association.

In 1950, she became the first black American to play in the U.S. Open, which was held at Forest Hills, N.Y. The next year, she achieved the same at Wimbledon in England.

Big Winner

When she won the U.S. Open and Wimbledon in 1957, she became the first black person to capture each title. Gibson repeated the sweep the next year and finished with 11 Grand Slam titles. She was inducted into the National Lawn Tennis Hall of Fame and the International Tennis Hall of Fame in 1971.

"(Gibson) simply changed the landscape of tennis," said Alan Schwartz, president of the U.S. Tennis Association, in the *Chicago Tribune*. "Arthur Ashe's job was not easy, but if he had to climb a hill, Althea Gibson had to climb a mountain. She was the original breakthrough person."

Gibson's life changed at the age of 13. While playing for fun on the Harlem River Tennis Courts, she caught the attention of a teacher named Juan Serrell. Serrell belonged to New York's prestigious black Cosmopolitan Club and arranged for Gibson to play tennis there. She impressed the members so much, they bought her a membership so she could start taking lessons from the club's pro players. The members' agenda was to promote black tennis players through the all-black American Tennis Association. By 1942, Gibson had entered and won her first of many ATA tournaments.

While her game was coming together, her life was in danger of coming apart. Gibson, still a minor, was a high school dropout with an unstable home life. But her tennis success caught the attention of two black doctors, Hubert Eaton and Robert Johnson, who promoted black tennis players. They had a plan to help her get an education and improve her game with an athletic scholarship to college.

To first gain a high school diploma, Gibson would live with Eaton and his family during the school year in Wilmington, N.C. In the summer, she'd live with Johnson and his family in Lynchburg, Va., while playing in ATA tournaments. Despite the incredible offer, in which all her expenses would be paid for, Gibson initially didn't want to leave the only world she knew in Harlem. She turned to her old friends, Robinson and his wife, Edna, for advice.

"I might have turned down the whole thing if Edna and Sugar Ray hadn't insisted that I should go. 'You'll never amount to anything just bangin' around from one job to another like you been doin',' Ray told me. 'No matter what you want to do, tennis or music or what, you'll be better at it if you get some education.' In the end I decided he was right," Gibson wrote in "I Always Wanted to Be Somebody."

Despite her spotty history at school, Gibson started studying with renewed vigor. She graduated high school at the advanced age of 22 in 1949.

Her grades and tennis skills earned her a full scholarship to Florida A&M University in Tallahassee, Fla. Gibson's tennis career and education came about because others cared about her, and she never failed to appreciate that.

"It was an amazingly generous thing for (Eaton and Johnson) to want to do, and I know I can never repay them for what they did for me," Gibson said. "No matter what accomplishments you make, somebody helped you."

Catching On

After dominating the women's ATA tournaments, Gibson caught the attention of the press and the white tennis establishment. Pressure was mounting on the U.S. Lawn Tennis Association for integration. Alice Marble, who'd been one of tennis' greatest players, wrote of the need for it in June 1950.

"If tennis is a game for ladies and gentlemen, it's also time we acted a little more like gentle people and less like sanctimonious hypocrites," Marble wrote.

When Gibson broke the color barrier at Wimbledon in 1951, she advanced to the third round. By 1953, she was ranked as the seventh-best player in the world, but in 1954 her poor performance in her first-round loss at Forrest Hills dropped her to 13th. *Jet* magazine called her "The Biggest Disappointment in Tennis." While she had conquered segregation in her sport, she had yet to win any USLTA tournaments.

With no professional women's tennis tour at the time, Gibson was struggling financially as an amateur player and as a physical education instructor at Lincoln University in St Louis. She was making only $2,800 a year. She began to get discouraged. "If I was any good (at tennis), I'd be the champ now. But I'm just not good enough," Gibson told one of her coaches.

Figuring she needed to try a different venue, she submitted an application to the Women's Army Corps. As a college graduate, she'd go in as an officer, receive a good salary and have a pension down the line.

Before enlisting, Gibson was offered the chance to be a part of a State Department goodwill tennis tour of Southeast Asia. She instantly changed her plans and spent hours surrounded with baskets full of tennis balls, experimenting with her stroke.

Her hard work and determination served her well. She won 16 of her 18 tournaments on the tour.

"The tour had renewed Gibson's enthusiasm for tennis. She would not give up on her game; instead, she resolved to do whatever was necessary to be the best," Tom Biracree wrote in "Althea Gibson."

After Gibson won Wimbledon in 1957, she received a ticker-tape parade in New York. Still, she remained humble.

"I have never regarded myself as a crusader," Gibson said. "I try to do the best I can in every situation I find myself in, and naturally I'm always glad when something I do turns out to be helpful and important to all Negroes — or, for that matter, to all Americans."

38

Basketball Coach
Phil Jackson

Focus On Teamwork Took His
Players To The Top

New York Knicks rookie forward Phil Jackson was goofing around with teammates on the bench during a game in the 1967–68 season.

Suddenly, Knicks coach Red Holzman was in Jackson's face. How much time was left on the 24-second shot clock? he demanded. Jackson didn't know.

He should, Holzman told Jackson: If Jackson was sent into the game without that information, it could cost the Knicks big.

The lesson? "Awareness is everything," Jackson said in "Sacred Hoops: Spiritual Lessons of a Hardwood Warrior," co-written with Hugh Delehanty.

Jackson used that lesson to help the Chicago Bulls win six National Basketball Association championships. In one of those seasons, 1995–96, the Bulls set the league mark for the best win-loss record in a regular season, 72-10. Based on his first nine seasons as a coach, Jackson owned the highest regular-season and playoff winning percentages of any NBA coach ever.

It's How You Play The Game

As head coach of the Los Angeles Lakers, Jackson teaches his players not to worry about winning or losing but to give their full attention to what's happening at the moment.

"To excel, you need to act with a clear mind and be totally focused on what everyone on the floor is doing," Jackson wrote.

Awareness is a concept Jackson has expanded through his study of Zen, which he combines with Christian values. In Zen philosophy, Jackson said, "all you need to do to reach enlightenment is to 'chop wood, carry water.'" What this means is to perform anything with "precise attention, moment by moment."

Jackson moved up from assistant to head Bulls coach in 1989. His goal was to win championships but not with a "win at all cost" mentality. His way wasn't yelling at players or being a control freak. He'd be strict, but would blend his love for basketball with his belief in the principles of selflessness and compassion.

"I had to take into account not only what I wanted to achieve but how I was going to get there," Jackson wrote.

Jackson wanted to form a team focused on working together, developing a group mentality that would become greater than the coaches or individual players. To foster this, Jackson drilled his players in the complex moves of the passing-based "triangle offense" — one player in front, with a player on either side forming the triangle, and two other players flanking them.

Because the triangle offense requires all five players to work in orchestrated unison, Jackson knew the approach would foster teamwork — "awareness in action," he calls it.

Jackson's philosophy regarding the triangle offense is that "if you look hard enough, you'll find (your opponent's) weaknesses."

Jackson's fellow assistant coach on the Bulls, Tex Winter, perfected the offense. Yet most other NBA coaches and players scoffed. With its roots in college basketball, the offense wouldn't work in the NBA, they said.

Bull superstar Michael Jordan was willing to consider the triangle offense, but hesitated. He felt some of his teammates couldn't make good decisions with the ball. Jackson realized the other players followed Jordan's lead. He knew he'd need to make sure Jordan was completely sold on the offense.

So when Jackson took over as head coach in 1989, he pointed out the advantages not only for the team but for Jordan as well. In his five-year career, Jordan had yet to win a championship. If his teammates got better, a championship was that much more likely, Jackson noted.

"You've got to share the spotlight with your teammates, because if you don't, they won't grow," Jackson told Jordan. Jordan saw the reasoning and immediately pledged his support.

"(Jackson) helped the greatest player to probably ever play understand a team concept," said B. J. Armstrong, who played with Jordan on three Bull NBA championship teams.

While training the Bulls in the intricate triangle offense, Jackson and Winter drilled the team over and over.

It showed. With the triangle in place, Jackson coached the Bulls to their six NBA championships.

Clearly Defined Principles

"Phil's . . . main objective as a coach is . . . preparing his team to focus under duress in a hostile environment," Armstrong said. "As a player, that's what I gained from him — being able to handle pressure situations and being able to make the responsible and right play on an opposing team's court in a seventh game (in a playoff series). If you're prepared for that situation, you'll do the right thing."

Jackson believes the most effective way to forge a winning team is to focus people on something larger than themselves. Then they have to decide that goal is what they all really want.

The Bulls, Jackson said, won championships because they "plugged in to the power of oneness instead of the power of one man," referring to the incomparable Jordan.

Jackson warns that once success is attained, the team must keep working together to improve. No one can focus too much on his own role.

"Success tends to distort reality and make everybody, coaches and players, forget their shortcomings and exaggerate their contributions," Jackson wrote.

"Success turns 'we's' back into 'me's,'" Jordan put it.

Jackson has clearly defined principles for his teams. He uses the principles to point out players' shortcomings on the court without making them feel singled out. He deals with problems in a manner that's "appropriate to the situation and causes no harm." He calls the approach "skillful means."

Jackson aims for what he terms "compassionate leadership." "This means treating everyone with the same care and respect you give yourself," he wrote.

One of his key tools is listening without judging. Jackson tries to look at players from their point of view.

In pressure situations, Jackson remains cool.

"I've never known anybody to handle crisis the way Phil does," Winter told Frank Deford in a Nov. 1, 1999, *Sports Illustrated* article. "He's able to read the big picture and not let the emotions of the moment control him."

Take a 1994 playoff game between the Bulls and the Knicks. With Jordan in his first retirement, Scottie Pippen was the Bulls' big star. With seconds left in a tie game, Jackson, during a timeout, bypassed Pippen for the game's last shot. Pippen was so upset he left the game, which the Bulls won on that shot.

Jackson knew coming down too hard on Pippen would only make a potentially explosive situation worse. He saw it as an isolated mistake by a frustrated Pippen. Jackson knew Pippen had never challenged his leadership before.

To deflate the situation, Jackson stepped back and allowed team leaders Bill Cartwright and Armstrong to express the team's disappointment right after the game to Pippen: he'd violated the Bulls' sacred code of selflessness. The approach was spot on — Pippen apologized to his teammates.

Thanks to Jackson's approach, Pippen repaired his relationship with the team. After Jordan ended his retirement in 1995, he and Pippen became again the key players on three more Bulls' championship teams. Pippen was named one of the NBA's 50 all-time greatest players in 1998.

Jackson works at keeping perspective. He once had such a burning desire to win as a player that "the obsession with winning had robbed me of my joy in the dance," he said.

Then he started searching for a different approach. After reading some Zen philosophy, he learned to accept losing as a step toward winning.

"Only by acknowledging the possibility of defeat can you fully experience the joy of competition. Winning is important to me, but what brings me real joy is being fully engaged in whatever I'm doing," Jackson explained. "Sometimes a well-played defeat will make me feel better than a victory in which the team doesn't feel especially connected."

39

Boxer Muhammad Ali
Dedication And Innovation
Helped Make Him A Champion

When Muhammad Ali (his name then was Cassius Clay) was just 12, people packed in to see his amateur fights even though he wasn't anything special as a fighter. Why did the crowds come?

One reason: his mouth.

Before each fight, he went door to door through his Louisville, Ky., neighborhood, introducing himself and telling people the date and time of the bout. If they weren't interested at first, once the youth finished a stream of rhyming boasts about how easily he'd win, they would be — if only to see him eat his words.

"I'd mouth off to anybody who would listen about what I was going to do to whoever I was going to fight," said Ali in "Muhammad Ali" by John Stravinsky. "People would go out of their way to come and see, hoping I would get beat. (They'd) start hollering. 'Bash in his nose!' or 'Button his fat lip!' I didn't care what they said as long as they kept coming to see me fight."

By realizing the value that a distinctive personality brings to an event, Ali would become arguably the best-known sports figure in the world during the 1960s and 1970s. His talent and dedication made him an Olympic and three-time professional heavyweight champion, but it was his charisma that kept fans most interested.

Total Study

Long before his glory days, he knew he'd have to work hard inside and outside the gym if he wanted to be a champion. So he dedicated his teen-age years to the total study of his sport.

Realizing that he needed more training than simply hitting the bags and sparring, he hung around the gym at all hours. He talked with old fighters about their techniques and quizzed trainers on the intricacies of the sport.

"I realized it was almost impossible to discourage him," said Joe Martin, a police officer who introduced the youth to boxing. "Even then he was a little on the smart-alecky side, but . . . he was easily the hardest worker of any kid I've ever taught."

To develop speed and stamina, he shadowboxed constantly in front of mirrors, woke at 5 a.m. daily to run and then raced the bus 28 blocks to school. He practiced foot racing against thoroughbred horses at Churchill Downs so much he got himself barred from the racetrack.

It wasn't that he loved the work regimen. He didn't. He simply realized the rewards it could bring.

"I hated every minute of the training," Ali recalled. "But I thought, 'Don't you quit. Suffer now and live the rest of your life as a champion.'"

Because only the most skilled trainers could teach him to succeed as a pro, he sought out the most respected in the business.

When renowned trainer Angelo Dundee came to Louisville in 1956 with one of his fighters, young Clay saw an opportunity to make an impression. But how would an unknown 14-year-old get time with Dundee?

Simple. He took the straightforward approach. He went to Dundee's hotel and called the room on the phone.

"This is Cassius Clay, the next heavyweight champion, talking," he said to Dundee. "I'm gonna win the Olympics and be the next heavyweight champ. I'm in the lobby. Can I come up?"

Dundee let him come up. Clay peppered him with three hours of questions about ring strategy and training secrets. Although he was still an amateur, the meeting jump-started a relationship in which Dundee agreed to train him when he turned pro four years later.

As a pro, he used the same tactics of his youth to publicize his early fights. To attract extra attention, he started calling the rounds he'd win before the fight. Fans attended to see whether his predictions came true, and at one point in 1962–63, he amazed audiences by getting it right in nine out of 10 fights.

Creative Marketing

Away from the ring, he kept up his self-promotion, reciting long poems about himself wherever he went — on television, at airports and at press conferences.

When then-champ Sonny Liston delayed in giving him a title shot, Clay didn't just quietly wait his turn. Instead, he hounded Liston night and day, calling for a match, according to "Muhammad Ali: Heavyweight Champion" by Jack Rummel.

In Las Vegas, Clay broke up Liston's blackjack game, shouting that he was the real champ. Then he interrupted Liston's craps game, catching the dice in mid-throw. Later, he showed up at Liston's Denver home early one morning, shouting he would "whip the champ." As he expected, the media picked up on the stunts, and when Liston finally gave in and fought him, Clay beat him to take the title.

Knowing that timing was crucial, he waited until the day after becoming heavyweight champ to announce his conversion to the Black Muslim faith. Although he had been an adherent for some time, he realized acceptance of his religion in racially torn America would be greater for a champion than for a defeated contender. He soon took the name Muhammad Ali.

Although the announcement hurt Ali's public image, he stuck to his beliefs, studying to become a Muslim cleric. Even when several endorsement deals fell through, Ali never considered compromising his values.

"A rooster crows only when it sees the light," Ali said. "Put him in the dark, and he'll never crow. I have seen the light, and I'm crowing."

As champ, Ali continued working to improve his skills, learning that only through increased innovation could he defeat new rivals. By holding his hands low, he found he could throw hooks quicker because he didn't have to pull his hands back first. He deceived opponents with an unprotected stance, luring them in close where they were easy targets.

Fighting George Foreman in 1974, Ali used his now-famous rope-a-dope technique, leaning deep into the ropes, letting Foreman tire himself out while Ali saved his strength for later.

If he lost a fight, as he did three times during the height of his career, he simply put it behind him and got ready for the next challenge.

"Just lost a fight, that's all," he said of his defeats. "Probably be a better man for it. You lose, you don't shoot yourself."

Occasionally, he underestimated an opponent, as he did with Leon Spinks in 1978. That cost him his title.

But for his rematch later that year, he immersed himself in preparation. Ali rented a secluded hideout on Lake Ponchartrain near New Orleans. In addition to his regular boxing workout, he ran an extra three to five miles every day. Each morning, he ate a regimented breakfast of two trout and eggs and toast without butter. He also took vitamin supplements regularly and did more than 8,000 sit-ups in a month and a half.

He won the rematch.

When Ali was drafted in 1967, he made a controversial decision to refuse to serve. Despite facing the loss of his title, charges of betraying his country and the possibility of up to five years in prison for violating the draft act, Ali decided he couldn't be a Muslim minister and a soldier at the same time.

"If I was in the service, I could not be teaching anything about the holy Koran," Ali said. "I'd be going against it. I'd be a hypocrite. If going to war, and possibly dying, would help 22 million blacks in this country gain freedom, justice and equality, I would join tomorrow."

He was stripped of his title and suspended from boxing for three years. But Ali stuck to his decision because he felt it was right.

"I still envy him," said basketball player Bill Russell. "He has something I have never been able to attain and very few people I know possess. He has absolute and sincere faith."

40

Baseball Executive Branch Rickey

His Vision And Courage
Integrated The Game

When Branch Rickey sensed an opportunity, he did everything he could to seize it — even if he had to wait 40 years for the opportunity.

In 1904, Rickey, then 22, played on and was the coach of the Ohio Wesleyan University baseball team. Upon checking the team into a South Bend, Ind., hotel for a game against Notre Dame, Rickey was told his lone black player, Charles Thomas, couldn't stay there.

Rickey stood up for Thomas, as he had many times before. But the accumulation of racial discrimination was taking its toll on Thomas. Sitting on a cot in Rickey's room, Thomas began sobbing.

"(Thomas) rubbed one great hand over the other with all the power of his body," Rickey recalled, "muttering, 'Black skin . . . black skin. If I could only make 'em white.' He kept rubbing and rubbing as though he would remove the blackness by sheer friction."

Rickey never forgot how prejudice could wound a man's spirit. He vowed that one day he'd find a way to fight back.

It took years, but Rickey (1881–1965) broke the race barrier in baseball; he also became known as one of the greatest front-office executives in baseball history. He was named to the Baseball Hall of Fame in 1967 in recognition of those achievements.

After a stint with the St. Louis Browns, Rickey was the front-office personnel mastermind behind four St. Louis Cardinal World Series championships and six pennants. He was with the Cardinals from 1917 to 1942, but figured that St. Louis was the wrong place to introduce a black player.

Then he got the call to become president of the Brooklyn Dodgers. In Brooklyn, Rickey saw a melting pot of many races.

"The very first thing I did when I came into Brooklyn in late 1942 was to investigate the approval of ownership for a Negro player," said Rickey in "Branch Rickey: A Biography" by Murray Polner.

New Navigation

Rickey had a great capacity for charting new waters, says his grandson, Branch B. Rickey, currently president of the Pacific Coast League. "Any issue that presented something worthwhile got great study," Branch B. Rickey said.

Once in Brooklyn, Rickey directed his scouts to find the right man in talent and temperament to break baseball's color barrier. In August 1945, he met Jackie Robinson, who was playing for the Negro League Kansas City Monarchs. Rickey knew Robinson was an excellent ballplayer, but Rickey had to be sure Robinson had the right personality, background, intelligence and desire.

Rickey didn't pull any punches. "The taunts and goads will be aimed at setting off a race riot in the ballpark," Rickey told Robinson. "Then they'll say that is proof that Negroes shouldn't be allowed in the major leagues."

To make sure Robinson could take abuse, Rickey role-played for three hours with him. Rickey yelled every disgusting racial taunt at Robinson he could think of. Every time Robinson reacted with normal anger, Rickey, a devout Christian and avid reader of the Bible, preached nonviolence.

"I get it, Mr. Rickey," Robinson finally said. "I've got another cheek. I turn the other cheek."

"No matter how vile the abuse, you must ignore it . . . and the day will come when every team in baseball will open its doors to Negroes," Rickey said.

After proving himself spectacularly in the minor leagues during 1946, Robinson broke the major-league color barrier on April 15, 1947. He valiantly put up with the abuse opponents and spectators gave him.

Rickey insisted his ballplayers show a unified front. When some of the Dodgers threatened to revolt in 1947, Rickey told them he'd trade any player who didn't want to play with Robinson.

"Mr. Rickey was an instrument in social change, and was prepared to initiate it, fight for it and stick with it when a lot of opposition developed," said Rachel Robinson, Jackie Robinson's widow, in a 2000 interview.

"My grandfather's approach as to the best way to eradicate bigotry, on a business model, was to discredit it by causing a very large success," Branch B. Rickey said.

Rickey tried to use every spare minute and typically worked 12 to 15 hours a day. "Rickey sometimes shaved in taxicabs and always abhorred any waste of time, money or energy," wrote Harvey Frommer in "Rickey & Robinson."

Winning Formula

A law school graduate who believed one's education never stopped, Rickey read continually. He owned and pored through volumes on Abraham Lincoln and other people he admired. He surrounded himself with portraits of Lincoln, Winston Churchill and Robinson in his office to remind him to strive for integrity and honor.

Rickey had a formula he followed for signing prospects. Everyday players had to have innate running and throwing ability. Pitchers had to have a good, natural fastball. All other skills and pitches could be learned, Rickey believed.

"Many thought (Rickey) was the greatest judge of talent in baseball history," Frommer wrote.

To receive maximum value in trades, Rickey kept detailed records on each of his players.

"You must know ahead of time who is failing," he said. "It is time to trade a player as soon as he reaches the twilight zone of stardom."

"Mr. Rickey was a visionary who could look and think ahead and see things that were needed. It allowed him to start a process in advance of the need," said Rachel Robinson.

Rickey looked for solutions well before problems reared their heads. After he started working with the Cardinals in 1917, Rickey wanted to figure out a way to build the struggling team into a powerhouse. At the time, minor-league teams were independent. They signed and developed players and sold them to the highest major-league bidder.

The Cardinals didn't have enough money to compete for the top athletes, so Rickey devised the farm system for developing players. In 1920 he bought the Texas League's Houston team for the Cardinals. Now the Cardinals could sign and train their own players there and promote them to the major-league club if they improved.

By 1928, the Cardinals owned seven minor-league clubs and had built an imposing team. Eventually, all major-league teams copied Rickey's model.

Yet Rickey stayed modest. "Starting the Cardinal farm system was no sudden stroke of genius," he said. "It was a case of necessity being the mother of invention."

He created a state-of-the-art home for spring training, Dodgertown, on a former Air Force base in Vero Beach, Fla., to ensure both major- and minor-league players got the best instruction. It was another of Rickey's attempts at careful planning.

"Luck is the residue of design," he often said.

To find the best prospects, Rickey developed a network of contacts throughout the country. "There wasn't a town in America where Rickey did not have some connection," Frommer wrote.

While most teams were cutting back on player development during World War II, Rickey wanted to build for the future. He increased his number of scouts fourfold.

"By the summer of 1943, . . . approximately 20,000 letters had been sent to high school coaches all over the United States asking them to recommend the best prospect available," Frommer wrote.

Out of that pool came players like star first baseman Gil Hodges and future Hall of Fame outfielder Duke Snider. The Dodgers won two National League pennants during Rickey's reign from 1942 to 1950. After he left for the Pittsburgh Pirates in autumn 1950, the Dodgers won four more pennants with the team he had put in place.

41

Skating Champ
Peggy Fleming
Perseverance Helped Her
Jump To The Gold

Peggy Fleming knew the difference between good and great —
and it was just 15 minutes.

When Fleming was 13 years old, she and another young skater
practiced every day at a local rink from 5 to 7 a.m. But Fleming realized that more practice time would let her improve more than the
other girl. So she began showing up 15 minutes early.

"The message you want to send your competitor is that you're
really serious about what you're doing and that you're going to work
harder than they are," Fleming said in a 1999 interview. "I already
knew that at 13."

Fleming rode that competitive spirit to glory, winning the figure
skating gold medal at the 1968 Winter Olympics in Grenoble, France.
She also won three world championships (1966–68) and five U.S.
national championships (1964–68). Her skill and daring on the ice
changed figure skating and inspired a generation of young skaters to
take up the sport. Experts consider her the most influential skater of
the 20th century.

Yet the San Jose, Calif., native began skating almost by accident,
as she wrote in her autobiography, "The Long Program."

Her mother noticed an advertisement in a paper for a new rink that offered special introductory prices. She immediately signed up Peggy, then just 9, for lessons.

Love What You Do

For Fleming, ice skating was an epiphany. She "found the one thing that made everything else fall into place," she wrote.

It was important that she loved skating — because loving something makes it easier to sacrifice for it.

She didn't love "getting up at 5 in the morning, getting to the rink before school, going to school all day before heading back to the rink after school, staying there until just before dinner, then doing homework before flopping into bed," Fleming said.

"It's just that I loved skating so much I was willing to pay the price," she said.

Before long, people were noticing her ability. In fact, Fleming won the first tournament she entered, a San Francisco-area juvenile event in 1959 at the age of 11.

Two weeks later she entered a larger competition, the Pacific Coast Championships, and learned a key lesson: Never assume anything.

She garnered her first victory in San Francisco so effortlessly she was convinced that's the way it would always be. Then she finished last in the PCC.

"I took (winning) for granted," she said. "This is fun. This is how you do it. When I lost, it was embarrassing. I didn't like it."

Fleming decided she'd never take another competition for granted. Instead, she practiced hard and then went through each of her moves mentally before stepping onto the ice.

"I learned to be nervous," she said.

Nerves are good, she maintains. Fear is not. Fear is just another emotion that must be conquered. She had confidence in her abilities. That approach saw her through the gamut of emotions she felt as she stepped onto the ice to compete.

"You have to believe in yourself and think positively," she said. "You focus on what you know you can do. You can do it if you believe you can.

"If you go out onto the ice with the attitude, 'Gee, I hope I don't fall,' you will fall. But if you go out and compete thinking, 'I've done this a million times in practice; what's one more time?' you'll make that jump."

Keep Growing

Even when she began winning regularly, Fleming wanted to keep growing in her sport.

Until her arrival in skating, competitors had crammed in as many moves as they could during their allotted time to impress judges with their skill. But Fleming wanted to make sure she stood out in competition.

So she put her own spin on her routines — she carefully choreographed her dramatic jumps, lunges and spins to music — as if she were doing a highly athletic dance. She made the sport as much about timing as athletics.

She was determined to skate to the beat of a different drummer. " 'There has to be more to it,' I remember thinking," Fleming wrote. "I always felt that skating could be more like art, if you could only find a way to put your whole self and your emotions into it and convey that to an audience."

When Fleming went to her first Olympics in 1964 at Innsbruck, Austria, she went face-to-face with the world's best skaters. Despite trying her hardest, the 15-year-old finished sixth. Yet she was far from discouraged.

Instead of dwelling on failure, Fleming studied the other competitors and found herself inspired by the superb athletes. "Having seen others do great things, I knew my own goals were achievable," she said.

Her goal? An Olympic gold medal of her own. To get it, she made up her mind that she'd never slack off — not even in practice. She went for perfection every time.

"By trying for perfection in my training, I was seeking to erase the line between practice and performance," Fleming said.

She understood that muscles remember how they perform a repetitive task. She resolved to train relentlessly until her muscles automatically remembered the right way to do a spin or jump.

She also studied and analyzed other skating programs and designed hers to fit her strengths.

"You have to learn to pace yourself," Fleming said. "You can't go full-out for four straight minutes. The program has to go in waves of energy and emotion, and I think that's a more fulfilling program for the judges to watch."

Typically, she began with some difficult moves, coasted for a while to regain her strength and then ended strongly.

Fleming focused on the big picture, but she didn't overlook the small details en route to her championships. She made sure her skates were polished every time she stepped on the ice. Before deciding on fabric for a costume, she'd ask a host of questions to figure out how it would affect her skating routine.

"Fabrics behave differently," she wrote. " 'If it has more weight to it, it will take longer for it to move — and to stop moving. You can do a turn or a spin and stop and the fabric will continue to wrap around you. To me, that is a look that builds excitement."

Bend, Don't Break

Of course, events don't always go according to plan. When that happens, she believes in being flexible — in picking herself up and continuing.

That's exactly what Fleming did in the 1967 World Championships.

Coming out of a jump, she inadvertently performed what she called her "butt slide." The fall could've cost her the title. Yet Fleming refused to allow that thought to deter her. She focused on finishing her routine perfectly and with a huge smile. She won the title.

"I trained myself that if something goes wrong, you just wash it out of your head and keep thinking positively," she said.

She also faces her problems head-on — before they become worse.

Take the time she and a friend were in the Galapagos Islands. Walking along the beach, the pair spied someone stealing the backpacks they'd left behind. The two women grabbed rocks and a spiky piece of cactus and took off after the thief. Eventually, they captured him and took him to town.

"Sometimes trouble seeks you out, and you can't walk away," Fleming wrote. "It's much better to confront it right away, before it wears you down."

That advice applies to more than muggers and purse snatchers. In January 1998, she found a lump on her breast. She immediately had it diagnosed and, when it proved to be cancer, treated. Following surgery and radiation treatment, she has remained cancer free — which she agrees is better than a gold medal.

42

Ivan Lendl's Grand Tennis Rise

He Slammed His Way To No. 1 With Mental And Physical Preparation

When it came to his tennis career, Ivan Lendl didn't leave anything to chance.

Early on his goal was straightforward: to become the best tennis player in the world. He'd even devised a simple formula to get there.

"My opinion is that if you are determined and work hard, anything is possible — or, put another way, nothing is impossible. But the faraway goal is not the real objective — the methodical day-to-day struggle is," Lendl said.

The struggle for tennis supremacy began in his native Czechoslovakia as the child of parents who were nationally ranked tennis players in their own right; his mother was ranked second, his father 15th. His parents introduced him to the game, but they didn't push him. Believing that he should pursue only a sport he liked, they presented tennis as an option.

It was young Ivan who did the pushing, relentlessly practicing and playing every chance he got. By the summer of 1984, after defeating John McEnroe in the French Open, Lendl was the No. 3-ranked player in the world.

Still not satisfied, Lendl made changes in his approach to complete his ascent. "I wanted to be No. 1," Lendl said in the foreword to Alexis Castorri's book "Exercise Your Mind: 36 Mental Workouts for Peak Performance." "So, following the (McEnroe) match, I made a commitment to myself to improve as many aspects of my game as possible. One of the things I did was to change my diet to improve my physical conditioning. Another thing I did was to begin working with Alexis to improve my mental conditioning (to focus better)."

Fit To Win

The increased conditioning, which Lendl called "the key to my success," paid off. In 1985, after defeating McEnroe in the U.S. Open, Lendl achieved tennis' No. 1 ranking. He held the position for 157 straight weeks and a record 269 weeks in total during his career.

At the time of his 1994 retirement, Lendl was tennis' all-time prizewinner, with $21,282,417. He also had a match record of 1,279-274.

Lendl won 94 singles titles (second to Jimmy Connors' 109), including eight Grand Slam crowns. He was named Association of Tennis Professionals Player of the Year in 1985, 1986 and 1987. He was inducted into the International Tennis Hall of Fame in 2001.

His focus has consistently been on becoming the best. "I don't like to lose in anything," he said.

For Lendl, tennis was his passion. "What kept me going, . . . what's allowed me to work so hard on improving my game, is the love I've always had for this sport. Everyone has dreams of glory, but if you want to realize those dreams, you've got to be able to put them aside while you work hard at something you love," Lendl wrote in "Hitting Hot" with George Mendoza.

Lendl embraced his practice time, and organized a detailed program with specific objectives. "Undirected, mindless practice is of no help whatsoever," he wrote. To that end, Lendl worked on his shots by setting up precise targets to aim for. "Use targets; the tangible proof of success will make more of an impact than just telling yourself you will hit to one of the corners of the service box," he said.

He also made time during his three-hour workouts to correct his weaknesses. "If there is one constant about my tennis life, it is practice. . . . The most important sort of practice is the practice you demand of yourself, when you make yourself go out and hit a certain stroke a hundred times, even if you'd rather be at home watching TV," Lendl said.

Still, he also preached balance. For Lendl, practice was regular and conducted with diligence but also kept fresh with necessary days off.

"I only practice when I want to. If you do otherwise, you're just kidding yourself," Lendl wrote in "Ivan Lendl's Power Tennis." "The session won't help at all if you're not keen. The best days for learning are those when you really want to play. You try new shots, you feel confident and you play well — and these factors reinforce themselves."

In match competition, Lendl put his opponents on the defensive and redefined tennis through his power game.

The virtue of such strategy was imparted on Lendl by his first coach, Olvrich Lerch.

"If you get a short ball or a clear shot at a winner, go for it. . . . In other words never push the ball when you can belt it," Lendl wrote.

"Lendl hits the forehand harder than anyone I've ever seen. . . . He deforms the ball when he hits it," said the late Arthur Ashe.

Having prepared himself physically for tournament play, Lendl worked to mentally ready himself. To free his mind of anxiety, he kept to the same eating and sleeping routine on the road as at home.

Before a match, Lendl focused on what shots he'd executed successfully in practice.

Realizing that forewarned is forearmed, Lendl studied his opponents and kept notes on all of them to understand their tendencies.

"The combination of your strengths and your opponent's weaknesses should dictate your game strategies," he said. "I have never stopped learning. Tennis constantly presents new challenges, both mental and physical."

Part of Lendl's strategy during a match was to stay in emotional control of himself and not let perceived bad calls affect him.

He also felt staying in control gave him a psychological edge against an opponent. "Any time you let your temper get the best of you, you lose the ability to concentrate on your game," he said.

Eyes On The Prize

"Concentration is critical to the extent that you never become preoccupied or distracted by things happening around you. When I say 'never take your eyes off the ball,' I'm not saying it's important to read its label, but it is crucial to follow the ball's flight from the opponent's hand to his service toss. It's not good enough to begin to watch the ball in midflight."

For all of Lendl's desire and will, he kept his career in perspective. "I have worked hard to get where I am. But I've enjoyed the journey," he said. "I think it's very important to remember that tennis is just a game — a beautiful, exciting game, to be sure, but nevertheless a game, something to be enjoyed and not suffered."

43

Driver
Michael Schumacher
He Races To Win

A race car driver's worst enemy is rain. Yet Formula One champion Michael Schumacher welcomes the challenge. Even as a young kart racer in Germany, Schumacher begged his coaches and track operators to let him drive in the rain.

Schumacher also admits he's most afraid of driving in the rain. Twice he's been caught in the spray from another car and crashed. Facing and conquering his fear help make Schumacher a great champion.

Schumacher, who drives for the famed Ferrari team, has dominated Formula One racing the past 10 years. He's won six world drivers' championships, surpassing the record previously held by legendary Argentine driver Juan Manuel Fangio, who had five drivers' championships.

For Schumacher, winning is everything.

"Michael is thinking every day, for much of the day, how to make himself better as a racing driver and what he can do to help make Ferrari better," said Frank Williams, head of the Williams team, in a 2002 *Time* magazine interview.

Schumacher's ability to drive to the limit all the time — especially in rainy conditions — is what sets him apart from the rest. In a TV interview with *60 Minutes*, Indy 500 champ Mario Andretti said Schumacher's talent lies in getting the best performance out of a car without going too far.

"Sometimes the Ferrari doesn't have to be the best car that particular day," he said. "But because he takes it to the limit, maybe he can make the car the best car that day anyway."

Mental Edge

Some say Schumacher's talent for getting the most out of a car was most evident when he drove for Benetton and won the drivers' title in 1994 and 1995. The Benetton car was widely considered inferior to the then-dominant Williams.

Schumacher paid no attention. He believed his car would perform well once he got behind the wheel.

Why? Because his edge is first and foremost a psychological one: He goes into every race expecting to win.

Sometimes Schumacher's superconfidence is seen as arrogance. That confidence is no doubt bolstered by his raw racing ability. A key characteristic of every great driver is the ability to lap at top speed from the second the light turns green at the start of a race. Schumacher ranks among the best in Grand Prix history in this department.

But his attitude is also based on solid hard work. He knows he's prepared well.

Schumacher started honing his talent from a young age. His father, Rolf, was a builder in Kerpin-Manheim, Germany, making a meager living. Yet when he saw his 4-year-old son's keen interest in go-karting, Rolf Schumacher made him a kart with an old lawn mower. Schumacher became the youngest member and driver at the local kart track.

When he was 5, his father built him a kart made from second-hand equipment. His whole focus was winning each race he entered. He won the championship that year even though his rivals were older and better equipped.

The rewards steadily increased. In 1984, Schumacher clinched the German Junior Kart Championship and held on to the title the next year.

He won every significant title every year until 1990, when he was recruited by Mercedes-Benz to race in the Sports World Championship.

Aware that top physical conditioning helps him keep his edge on the race course, Schumacher's fitness regimen is legendary. Other drivers try to emulate him. Few stick to it. Schumacher exercises up to four hours a day. He swims, runs, bikes, stretches and works out on machines. Many of his friends have joked that when he goes running with his dog, it's the dog that tires first.

Most of Schumacher's exercises focus on strengthening his neck to fight the G-forces of the incredible speeds he drives nearly every day. Schumacher's old fitness guru, Harry Haweika, has said Schumacher has to be in great shape every day, not just race day, because the car goes just as fast in practice as it does on race day.

Schumacher also follows a strict diet. He rarely eats sweets and doesn't drink alcohol.

Keeps It In Perspective

So has Schumacher's confidence ever been tested or shaken? Absolutely. Did he think of quitting? Yes. In the 1999 British Grand Prix, Schumacher's brakes failed as he approached a corner. He plowed into a wall at more than 160 kilometers per hour. The impact broke his car's chassis and his right leg.

Recovery was long and hard. He was unable to drive for three months. But Schumacher couldn't resist the lure of the challenge of getting back into the races.

"Nobody wants to die," he said in the *60 Minutes* interview. "We don't do it for the thrill of danger. We do it for the thrill of speed, being at the limit."

Schumacher understands that car racing's a team sport. So he takes time to get to know the team in the pit and garages. He listens to their advice, and never misses a chance to pay tribute to them when he's standing on the winner's podium.

Schumacher's deep knowledge of car mechanics stems from his school days. While he excelled in karting, he knew the importance of learning a variety of subjects and stayed in school. After finishing high school, he took up an apprenticeship at a local garage.

He keeps looking for new driving techniques even now. When he isn't preparing for a race, he's trying out new equipment at Ferrari's test track in Fiorano, Italy.

"Formula One is not just about driving," Schumacher said in a 2001 *BusinessWeek* interview.

In order not to burn out, Schumacher turns to his family to balance his frenetic work schedule. He retreats to his home in Switzer-
land and plays with his two kids. He runs and cycles around the
village and plays soccer for the local team.

"When I'm at home, I'm put back into a normal world, jumping
on the trampoline with the kids. . . . It helps me be balanced, and
that's important," he told *Time*.

His strategy has paid off. As of 2004, Schumacher is the highest
paid race driver in history, earning an estimated $50 million a year,
including merchandising and endorsements. And Schumacher has
led Ferrari back to its former glory.

PART 6

Fine-Tuning Focus Yields Excellence

© Reuters/CORBIS

When you compete against someone of equal or greater ability, it can lift your energy and mental concentration to new heights. A certain degree of positive stress can be very beneficial and can motivate you to work harder. The key is to see your rivalry as your guiding light, as a tool you can use to find the potential within yourself.

— Paula Newby-Fraser

44

Basketball Coach "Red" Auerbach

He Shot For The Best To Make Sure His Team Came Out On Top

A rnold "Red" Auerbach didn't care a hoot about the next-best player available in the National Basketball Association draft. He wanted only the best for the Boston Celtics.

"If a player doesn't have the right attitude, he isn't going to play for the Boston Celtics. Period. Attitude is always more important to me than ability," Auerbach stressed in his 1991 book, "MBA: Management by Auerbach."

In fact, Auerbach would look for players others overlooked. He'd look ahead when others looked back — all in the quest for Celtic victories and upholding Celtic pride.

Auerbach, born Sept. 20, 1917, wouldn't depend on statistics to measure players. "Stats are the most overrated thing in sports as far as I'm concerned," Auerbach wrote. "There are too many factors that can't be measured. You can't measure a ballplayer's heart, his ability to perform in the clutch, his willingness to sacrifice his offense or to play strong defense."

Auerbach's results speak for themselves. His nearly half-century run with the Celtics resulted in nine championships as coach from 1950 to 1966 and seven as the team's top front-office man since 1966. He won 1,037 games in 20 seasons, and the NBA Coach of the Year award was named after him.

Teams, Not Stars

As a coach and general manager, Auerbach disdained a pro-sports star system. Instead, he went about building championship teams whose reign defined eras.

In addition to wanting the best players, as he defined them, Auerbach wanted their best performances and their best appearances to show the world they were serious about winning. He insisted that his Celtics wear coats and ties on the road and play with their shirts tucked in. During timeouts, they remained standing.

While he demanded their all, he gave them his all in return. There was, for instance, the way Auerbach took on referees. If he thought they made a bad call against his players, he'd berate them mercilessly.

Auerbach didn't just want his players to be great — he wanted to make sure they worked well as a team.

"You had a lot of great players with different personalities," said John Havlicek in a 1999 NBA.com online interview. "He was able to blend that situation to where everyone realized that they were paid based on their value to the team — not on how many points they scored, how many rebounds they had."

After four seasons as coach with the Washington Capitals, Auerbach joined the Celtics as head coach in 1950. The Celtics led the league in assists in 1950–51 and ranked near the top in points per game. But early in that season's playoffs, New York stung Boston by sweeping the series.

The Celtics' postseason losing pattern would repeat itself for several years.

Think Like A Winner

To halt that pattern, Auerbach decided he had to change his players' mental focus. He repeatedly told the players that they were winners.

He still does. In January 1999, he told forward Antoine Walker, "Hey, you're the captain. Act like one. Be in control."

Auerbach wanted players to concentrate on their strengths, not the other team's weaknesses.

"In fact, most of the time, when I was playing for Red, we never scouted the other team," Bill Russell said in a 1999 online chat session, "because our attitude was (one) of total and complete arrogance. We know what we're going to do; let them figure out how to counter us."

Auerbach's positive-thinking strategy also helped psych out opponents.

"Red believed, like the Marine Corps, in destroying the will of the other team to beat you," said Tom Heinsohn, a teammate of Russell and later the Celtic coach. "He just kept coming at people and made it a true physical and mental test to beat us."

Willing To Negotiate

Auerbach understood that to get what he wanted, he'd have to be willing to negotiate. Take his drafting of Russell in 1956.

Few others in the league took serious interest in Russell. Drafting black players in a time of rising racial tensions might hurt gate receipts. Besides, Russell lacked the offensive skills that helped attract crowds. His defense, however, transformed any basketball game.

Rochester owner Lester Harrison had a draft choice before Auerbach, though, and might have had his eyes on Russell.

Auerbach decided to find something he could trade with Harrison to be sure of drafting Russell. He knew that then-Celtics owner Walter Brown owned the Ice Capades and that Harrison wanted the skating troupe to appear in his arena.

Auerbach had Brown broker a deal — two weeks of the Ice Capades in Rochester in exchange for Harrison's pledge not to draft Russell ahead of the Celtics.

Harrison accepted. Eight straight league titles followed.

To make a player look especially attractive, Auerbach knew how to use reverse psychology.

At one point as general manager, Auerbach found himself with league scoring champ Bob McAdoo on the Celtics. McAdoo had been hired by new owner John Y. Brown without Auerbach's agreement. Auerbach was livid.

After Brown was bought out several months later, Auerbach decided he wanted to acquire Detroit Piston guard M. L. Carr, wrote Dan Shaughnessy in "Seeing Red: The Red Auerbach Story." He saw that Detroit could use McAdoo.

So Auerbach let it be known that McAdoo was off-limits. Detroit took the bait. Auerbach agreed to a deal in the summer of 1979 that included giving up McAdoo for Carr.

Larry Bird would later say that Carr was the soul of the Celtics' 1984 championship team, even though he wasn't part of the starting lineup.

45

Triathlete
Paula Newby-Fraser
She Became The Best By
Keeping Her Mind Clear

Eight-time Hawaii Ironman Triathlon champ Paula Newby-Fraser doesn't do warm-up runs the day before a race. She doesn't walk the course, or study local maps and ocean currents.

Instead, she gets her mind ready by reading romance novels.

There aren't any secrets for success hidden in bodice rippers. But the books do give her a much-needed mental break before an important race.

"Reading fiction bestsellers transforms me away from the world of fast-paced training and competition," she said in her book, "Peak Fitness for Women." "It's my way of blanking out worrisome thoughts about the future and bringing my mind back to the present. For me, thinking and worrying about the future takes a tremendous amount of energy."

By saving up her energy, Newby-Fraser has won the Hawaii Ironman — a combined 2.4-mile ocean swim, 112-mile bike ride and 26.2-mile run — more times than anyone else. The Los Angeles Times named her Professional Female Athlete of the decade in 1989, and that same year, ABC's *Wide World of Sports* called her the Greatest All-Around Female Athlete in the World. In 1990, the Women's Sports Foundation presented her with the Professional Sportswoman of the Year award.

Sought Challenges

It all started as a hobby. Back in her hometown of Durban, South Africa, Newby-Fraser, born June 2, 1962, never thought of herself as a jock. She worked a 9-to-5 job, went shopping and spent weekends at the beach working on her tan.

When a friend invited Newby-Fraser to go running in 1983, she thought, "Why not?"

After a few months, Newby-Fraser was hooked, and started pushing herself to go faster as she ran. Looking for an even greater challenge, she added swimming and bicycling. She practiced each sport relentlessly, for hours every day.

It paid off. Three years after that first run, she entered her first Hawaii Ironman and took first place.

Even after she became a professional athlete, she found she worked better if she made sure she was always having fun.

"In the races where I've done best, many of which have been in Hawaii, there's no other way to describe it than to say it felt effortless," she said.

To combat the pressures that come with competing for a living, Newby-Fraser tries to make her job feel like a hobby.

For example, to keep herself relaxed and free of expectations while she races, she never wears a watch.

"I'm going out there for the feeling," she said. "I may be out there for nine hours, but sometimes it feels like 90 minutes. Someone in the transition area might say, 'Oh, the leader is two minutes ahead.' But in my mind they may as well have said, 'Oh, the sun is shining.' Because I refuse to be ruled by the clock, the mental hardship is minimized."

Before a race, Newby-Fraser tries not to allow herself to get stuck in the trap of comparing herself to others. At prerace meetings, she makes every effort to switch off any thoughts such as "She looks fitter than I am."

"When I make comparisons at these meetings, there's usually a snowball effect," she said. "The comparisons linger in my mind up to the day of the race. I don't do as well as I'd hoped."

Instead, Newby-Fraser uses rivals to improve herself. "When you compete against someone of equal or greater ability, it can lift your energy and mental concentration to new heights," she said. "A certain degree of positive stress can be very beneficial and can motivate you to work harder. The key is to see your rivalry as your guiding light, as a tool you can use to find the potential within yourself."

Part of developing a healthy rivalry is hoping your rivals get better. Why? "Instead of wishing a competitor ill fortune, the healthy athlete wants a rival to succeed so that they can both rise to a whole new level," she said.

Newby-Fraser also tries to stay away from the dreaded "what ifs." Instead, she discards negative mental phrases and rewires her brain for success.

For example, if she begins filling her head with thoughts like "What if I don't win?" or "What if I don't finish?" she merely replaces the "What if?" with a "So what?" Her thoughts then shift to "So what if I don't win?" or "So what if I don't finish?"

Yet it's important not to get too confident, she's found. Five hundred yards from the finish of the 1995 Hawaii Ironman, dehydration and heat exhaustion overcame Newby-Fraser.

Earlier that day, several minutes in the lead, she'd gotten so carried away with her success that she started passing up water stations without drinking. Eventually, her body simply couldn't go any further, and, finish line in sight, she collapsed by the side of the road.

As her foes sped by, Newby-Fraser wondered if her days at the top had come to an end. Finally, pulling together all of her strength, she got up and hobbled to the finish line for fourth place.

"Crawling," she later said, "was not an option."

Afterward, Newby-Fraser decided she had to confront her feelings of failure and doubt to move past them. She had to get rid of the sick feelings that come with disappointment and learn exactly what her mistakes were.

Put It In Writing

Newby-Fraser began putting her professional mistakes in writing. Drawing a line down the center of a piece of paper, she recorded all of the facts about her latest mess-up, including her speed, her heart rate, the weather and what she did or didn't eat.

On the right side of that paper, she wrote down her feelings during the failed race. If she felt like crying, she jotted it down. If she was angry, she made a note of it.

It's a practice she continues. By separating the feelings from the facts, Newby-Fraser is able to distance herself from the messy situation so she can get something useful out of it. "That's a big step in making a comeback," she insists.

Once back in the game, it becomes crucial to think about right now — not what happened before or what will happen after the race.

To keep herself focused, Newby-Fraser will zone in on her movements one at a time, checking to make sure she is performing each one to the best of her ability. Instead of worrying whether she'll win, Newby-Fraser ensures she's pedaling in perfect circles, or breathing evenly.

Challenges are best met if you "keep your mental focus on something very specific and tangible," said Newby-Fraser.

In the 1996 Hawaii Ironman Triathlon, Newby-Fraser flew across the finish line in first place — her eighth championship in the Kona, Hawaii, race. As she ran the last three miles, she shielded herself from any bad memories by repeating to herself, "Now is all there is." That same year, Newby-Fraser was named to the Ironman Hall of Fame.

46

Golf Champ Nancy Lopez

Focus And Positive Attitude
Helped Her Win Championships
And Fans' Hearts

She's known for her beaming smile, but there were tears in Nancy Lopez's eyes that Sunday in July 1997.

Lopez had just suffered a one-stroke defeat in the U.S. Open at the Pumpkin Ridge Golf Course in Cornelius, Ore.

It was her fourth runner-up finish in the tournament, which was the only major she didn't win. Still, Lopez took her seat afterward in the press room — something some golfers aren't willing to do following a loss.

When asked how she felt, she wiped her eyes. Her answer: The close score taught her that she was capable of winning that tournament. She took a loss and turned it into a personal lesson.

"I was blown away by the mental toughness and the wisdom of Nancy Lopez," said Leslie Day Craige, editor in chief of *Golf For Women* magazine. "The way she handled that defeat was a defining moment in her career as an extraordinary person and top-level competitor."

That combination of collegiality and strength characterizes Lopez. Her career is marked not only by outstanding golf skills but also by her consistently positive, professional attitude, including her trademark grin.

"If you win or lose, your expression shouldn't change much," Lopez said in a 2001 interview. "That's what my mom and dad instilled in me." Along with giving a 100% effort in each tournament, her goal is to be a good winner and be a good loser.

In a career that lasted almost 25 years, she won nearly 50 titles beginning with a stunning win in the New Mexico Women's Amateur Championship at age 12. Lopez is a four-time Rolex Player of the Year winner and a three-time Vare Trophy winner for lowest scoring average. She also won the 1978 Ladies Professional Golf Association's Rookie of the Year award. She's the only woman to win LPGA Player of the Year, Rookie of the Year and the Vare trophy in the same season. She was the youngest player ever inducted into the LPGA Hall of Fame, in 1987.

Good Graces

She did it all with good manners, winning legions of fans in the process.

"She's very generous with her time," said Don Wade, who co-authored a book of golf anecdotes with Lopez. "The only complication of working with Nancy is that if anyone wanted an autograph, everything waited until she gave it."

When 19-year-old Lopez burst onto the professional women's golf scene in the late 1970s, it was a man's game. For women, sponsorship money was hard to come by, and so was public interest. Only diehard fans followed the women. The media wrote almost exclusively about male champs, such as Jack Nicklaus.

Lopez's debut changed things. She achieved a streak of five wins in a row and nine tour victories in 1978. The press and just about everybody else took notice of Lopez and her peers on the tour from then on.

"She was to women's golf what the Beatles were to popular music," wrote the editors of *Golf Digest*. "Her nine victories in 1978 put the LPGA on everyone's map." And her five-tourney streak put Lopez on the cover of *Sports Illustrated*.

Lopez had long focused on trying to be the best. She first picked up a club at age 8 with guidance from her father, Domingo. Hooked immediately, Lopez vowed to dedicate herself to mastering the game.

It wasn't easy. She grew up in remote Roswell, N.M. Lopez's father owned an auto body shop, and money was tight. But her determination was catching, and her parents were as devoted as she. They scraped together their money to afford Nancy's game fees.

They also taught her that how she handled herself was as important as how she handled her game. Wanting her daughter to put her best foot forward before she stepped on the green, her mother made sure Nancy had a new outfit each time she played a tournament, says Wade.

Lopez learned humility and hard work from her parents. Those traits worked in tandem with her ability to focus and her drive to win.

Former Olympic skater Bonnie Blair noted in *Golf Digest* that Lopez has a "fierce intensity" that's rare in sports.

Said Lopez: "My mom always told me if I didn't do it right, then I was wasting my time."

Despite her many achievements, Lopez strives to stay down to earth. "Lots of times athletes lose that," she said. "They don't remember where they come from, and they make themselves bigger than anybody around them."

Total Focus

Concentration on a task is crucial, and Lopez has it in spades. "When I am out there playing, I focus totally," she said.

Just as important is the mental rest she takes between shots, when she walks the course. "I think if I had to focus for the whole 4½ hours, it would have been really tough to do that," she said.

Lopez supports the game both on and off of the course. She's an avid supporter of AIM, a nonprofit group that uses music and movement to help handicapped people, and she serves as a playing editor for *Golf For Women*. In addition, she's developed her own line of golf gear.

Unlike some athletes today, Lopez wants to be a role model and pass along some of what she's learned, says Wade. She mentors younger players, including Korea's Se Ri Pak, who's been quoted as saying she wants to be "just like Nancy Lopez."

"She is still the most recognized and marketable women's golfer out there," said Craige.

While she loves to win, Lopez strives most of all for integrity. It wasn't long ago, in 1998, that Lopez won the prize she says means the most to her: the USGA's Bob Jones Award for distinguished sportsmanship.

"To me that's what my whole career is all about. It's what I wanted to do as a professional athlete, to have that kind of recognition as a player," she said.

In March 2002, Lopez announced that year — her 25th LPGA Tour season — would be her final full season on the tour. The remainder of that year was known as the "Nancy Lopez Farewell Tour."

Knowing when to step back is crucial to success, and Lopez decided that 2002 was the year to change her focus from competition to development. And change is good, Lopez says.

"I am at the beginning of a brand new chapter in my golf career," she said, noting that she's now concentrating on commentating, golf course design and her namesake club line.

Balance is also paramount, Lopez knows, and her scaled-back travel schedule means she'll get to spend more time with husband Ray Knight, the former baseball player, and their three daughters.

47

Sprinter
Florence Griffith Joyner
She Trained Her Mind As Hard
As She Did Her Body

Florence Griffith Joyner would be on the track, eyes forward, running a 600-meter sprint. Running right behind her would be her coach and husband, Al.

If she slowed just an instant, she'd hear him whisper, "I'm going to pass you."

And she'd be off.

Over and over, he'd whisper. Over and over, she learned to hit the afterburners, to release the kick that helped make her the world's top female sprinter.

Running, she said, was a mental game.

At the 1988 Olympics, she burst out of the pack, devastating her opponents. She won gold medals in the 100- and 200-meter sprints and the 400-meter relay, and a silver medal in the 1,600-meter relay. Her time in the 200 meters (21.34 seconds) and her Olympic trial time for the 100 meters (10.49) stand as world records.

Her performance was so stunning that many were certain she was taking steroids. But Griffith Joyner, who died Sept. 21, 1998, at the age of 38, always tested clean.

Staying Loose

Understanding how much the mind figured into her race, the Los Angeles native learned to exert tremendous control over her style.

"She was able to control the effort so that it was still relaxed and therefore efficient," said Bert Lyle, coordinator of women's sports development for USA Track & Field in Indianapolis.

Joyner knew strict discipline from the time she was a child. She grew up one of 11 children in a housing project in the Watts section of Los Angeles.

Outside were drugs and crime. Inside, their divorced mother kept a close watch on the children. She didn't allow them to watch television during the week, called for lights out at 10 p.m. and required them to discuss their wrongdoings with the Bible as their guide.

Florence, who inherited her mother's feisty, independent spirit, looked back on the discipline with appreciation.

"Everybody in the family survived. Nobody does drugs; nobody got shot at," she once said. "I used to say it was because we were afraid of Mama's voice. We didn't know how poor we were. We were rich as a family."

"When I was growing up, my mother was willing not to eat so that we could. Sometimes Mama would get this gaze in her eyes, and I'd ask her what she was thinking about. She'd say, 'I just want to get you guys out of here. This is not a home.' I couldn't understand that until I got older," she once told *Newsweek*.

Griffith Joyner's father was equally strict. When she visited him on weekends at his home in the Mojave Desert, he'd drill her on using proper diction.

She'd return to Watts, speaking softly and distinctly, using meticulous enunciation to disguise a slight lisp. Others teased her that she was different. But she soon learned to use her distinctiveness.

Made Herself Feel Special

She dressed unusually, wore different-colored socks and twirled her hair into various piled-up styles to feel good about herself. Before long, while the other kids taunted her, she was cleaving to a strong sense of self.

It was that same sense of self that propelled her onto the Olympic track, wearing 6-inch, spangled fingernails, one-legged bodysuits she designed herself and the certainty that she'd leave all the other runners in her wake.

She credited her parents for helping instill that mental toughness: "I have a strong foundation from my parents. That always taught me that sticks and stones may break my bones, but names will never hurt me. That prepared me mentally, on and off the track."

It was also as a child that Griffith Joyner decided she'd become a great runner. Visiting her father in the desert, she'd not only chase, but also catch jackrabbits.

She ran in high school and college, and competed in the 1984 Los Angeles Olympics, where she was a silver medalist in the 200-meter sprint.

She was frustrated by the decision to leave her off the U.S. 400-meter relay team, which won a gold medal. But she quickly used the emotion to motivate and inspire herself to train harder.

In fact, in the year preceding the 1988 Olympics, "She worked the hardest of any sprinter I've ever known," Lyle said.

The 5-foot-6, 130-pounder would train for five hours every day. She not only trained hard, but also trained smart. She analyzed the different aspects of sprinting and trained for each.

Take how she developed her fast "ground time." The most crucial part of sprinting, ground time measures how long the foot is on the ground.

Every day, she'd take a jump rope and train herself to take quick steps, Lyle noted. She jumped rope so rapidly her heel wouldn't touch the ground (sprinters want only the ball of the foot hitting the track).

Her ground time? Nine-hundredths of a second, "less than any female sprinter we know of," Lyle said.

Investing In Herself

To train the rest of her body, she ran repetitively in place, lifting her thighs until they were parallel to the ground. She lifted weights to strengthen her hamstrings and buttocks. She ran sprints of various lengths and sometimes in a set number of strides, such as 10 meters in 30 strides or 20 meters in 60 strides.

In addition to all this, she supported herself by working at a bank.

"Every day I tell myself I'm not going to allow anything to stop me," she once said. "I try to see my goals before me. There are a lot of things which could try to knock me down — injuries, family problems, financial problems, but you have to be so mentally tough when you're out there."

At the Olympics, Griffith Joyner's muscles and kick were so strong that rumors swirled about performance-enhancing drugs.

While other athletes might have wilted under such pressure, she handled the controversy in a sophisticated and classy manner, winning over the media with her positive demeanor and receptiveness to interviews. She also was accommodating to the public, often signing autographs for hours when asked by fans.

"She never showed a hint of impatience or intolerance or disgust," said Terry Crawford, the U.S. women's track coach for the 1988 Olympics. "She really extended herself to people when obviously her thoughts were preoccupied with her own personal goals and what she was trying to accomplish."

After retirement, she lived other dreams of her youth. She designed clothes, including the uniforms of the National Basketball Association's Indiana Pacers, and was selected in 1993 as co-head of the President's Council on Physical Fitness.

"I feel like I am a survivor," she once said. "You never fail until you stop trying."

48

Basketball Legend
Michael Jordan

Discipline And Desire Made Him
Synonymous With Success

If you want to be like Mike, you have to think like Mike.

That's because Michael Jordan's greatest gift isn't his physical ability, but rather his mental discipline. He was determined from the start to fully maximize his natural talent.

"Success . . . is something you have to put forth the effort for constantly; then maybe it'll come when you least expect it. Most people don't understand that," Jordan said.

"Anyone can be like Mike. . . . Whatever your field, you can do it. (Jordan) is a normal guy. He just works harder than anyone else," NBC sportscaster Ahmad Rashad, one of Jordan's closest friends, said in "How to Be Like Mike: Life Lessons About Basketball's Best" by Pat Williams with Michael Weinreb. Williams is the senior vice president of the Orlando Magic.

Jordan's practice habits and conditioning regimen amount to an "almost alarming harshness," Williams wrote.

"Michael Jordan is discipline. Not some of the time. Not most of the time. All of the time," said former Chicago Bulls teammate B.J. Armstrong.

The third leading scorer in National Basketball Association history with 32,292 points, Jordan won the NBA scoring title a record 10 times. His 30.1 career regular-season scoring average is first in NBA history, as is his 33.4 career playoff scoring average. Jordan was voted the league's Most Valuable Player five times and the NBA Finals' MVP six times. In 1999 he was selected as one of the 50 Greatest Players in NBA history.

Regardless of the heights he reached, Jordan was never satisfied. "I was aware of my success, but I never stopped trying to get better," Jordan said.

Hitting The Jumper

He went from being an average defensive player to one named eight times to the NBA's All-Defensive First Team. His jump shot was considered a weakness when he came into the NBA, so he regularly stayed late after practice working on it. Jordan says it took him until his fourth NBA season to become a pure shooter. His career field-goal percentage was a remarkable .497.

"His development was grounded in principles; it wasn't otherworldly, much as he could make it look so," said the legendary Dean Smith, Jordan's coach at the University of North Carolina.

Williams, a veteran personnel expert who built the Philadelphia 76ers into a championship team as their general manager, put the relationship between Jordan's natural talent and his effort this way: "Without the ceaseless work ethic, Jordan is merely another talented athlete gliding through an admirable career, but nothing historic."

Jordan was more than a scorer. He was a leader who took his Bulls to six NBA titles in the 1990s.

"I have no individual goals. We play for one reason, and that's to win the title," Jordan told his teammates before each season.

"M.J. is the ultimate one-on-one player, yet he understands that winning big is determined by involving his teammates," said Orlando Magic forward Grant Hill, a Jordan rival.

Jordan calls practice "more important than the game." Chicago teammates remember he was early at practice and the last to leave.

Over the course of the long, grueling NBA season, Jordan didn't look ahead to the playoffs. He played one game at a time, quarter by quarter.

"The thing that makes Michael who he is," Armstrong said, "is his focus. His ability to concentrate absolutely. To set everything else aside other than what needs to be done right now."

Williams said: "Jordan had no tolerance for lapses — from teammates, from coaches, from anyone. He understood the detriment, even the danger, of divided focus."

Jordan kept himself in a positive frame of mind and became one of the greatest clutch players in NBA history. He said he just did in games what he'd practiced "a million times."

"I never looked at the consequences of missing a big shot," Jordan said. "Why? Because when you think about the consequences, you always think of a negative result."

Win or lose, Jordan would analyze games, but he didn't allow them to linger. "I play the game over in my mind and get out of it what I can. I'll think about it for a while, then let it go," he said.

When Jordan was a high school freshman, he was cut from the varsity basketball team and sent to the junior varsity. He learned a lesson from the experience. "Getting cut was good, because it made me know what disappointment felt like, and I knew I never wanted to have that feeling, ever again . . . that taste in my mouth, that hole in my stomach," Jordan said.

Jordan's immediate goal then wasn't to play in the NBA — it was only to make the varsity team the next year. "I kept my dreams closer to me, and more realistic. One step at a time. . . . I can't see any other way of accomplishing anything," he said.

Jordan, who returned to basketball with the Washington Wizards in 2001 after three years in retirement, believes in staving off discouragement. "Obstacles don't have to stop you. If you run into a wall, don't turn around and give up. Figure out how to climb it, go through it or work your way around it," Jordan said.

Jordan works to be professional. Williams wrote that every night of Jordan's career, he wore a suit before and after the games. He's friendly to the media and the fans.

Considerate And Generous

"(Jordan) was always so aware of other people's feelings," said *Chicago Sun-Times* sportswriter Rick Telander. "He set the standard for superstar conduct, period."

Then there's Jordan with charities. "(Jordan) hugs, he talks, he takes up twice the time allotted by the publicists and the agents for the Make-A-Wish (Foundation) children, until both (he and the children) are nearly in tears," Williams wrote.

Doug Collins, who coached Jordan in Chicago and Washington, wrote in the foreword of Williams' book, "When reflecting on M.J., these words immediately come to mind . . . ultimate competitor, quintessential example, punctual, prepared, respectful."

Regardless of your profession, Collins wrote, "Apply (Jordan's) characteristics to your daily regimen, (and) you will be preparing yourself to perform at a championship level."

49

Baseball Great
Satchel Paige
Focus Kept Him Aiming High

Satchel Paige knew that the best way to slide one by batters was to keep them off balance. And the best way to do that was to keep them guessing.

Paige (1906–82), considered the greatest pitcher in the Negro Leagues and one of the best in baseball history, perfected a blistering fastball that looked like fire, according to one player. He delivered it time after time with near-flawless control.

Hitters sensed that the fastball was coming, but Paige worked to keep them guessing with a creative assortment of windups and releases. He never threw the same way on consecutive pitches.

Paige's ability to outwit batters was evident in his extended career from 1926 to 1967. Most of that period was in the Negro Leagues, where he compiled such feats as 64 straight scoreless innings, 21 straight wins, and 32-7 and 31-4 records. He posted an unofficial 2,000 wins, 300 shutouts and 55 no-hitters. He was inducted into the National Baseball Hall of Fame in 1971.

Intimidating Arsenal

Paige was known as the "man with a thousand windups," an arsenal he used to intimidate batters. His most famous one was the "hesitation" pitch. The right-handed pitcher paused for a split second in mid-delivery, suspended his left foot in midair and released the ball.

Overeager batters often swung before the ball left his hand, becoming half-corkscrewed into the ground by the time they swung and missed.

To vary his delivery, Paige developed single-, double- and triple-windup pitches. He'd often wind his arm in as many as seven revolutions before whipping the ball toward the plate. As one sportswriter put it, "He winds up in the old-fashioned, arm-cranking style that went out with the electric automobile."

To give himself an assortment from which to choose, Paige used different releases. He might throw in a straight overhand form on his first pitch to a batter and whip the ball sidearm next. On the third pitch, he might pump quickly toward the plate from a three-quarters position and throw a submarine pitch on the next one.

"Everyone knew what was coming, but they didn't know where it was gonna be," Paige told an interviewer. "If you're looking for it here, and I throw it up there, it's too late — you can't get back up there to hit it. I would tell 'em where I was gonna throw it. They still couldn't hit it."

Paige knew he couldn't succeed with his fastball alone. So he practiced with different throwing styles until he expanded his repertoire. The two best — a change-up known as his "soft pitch" and a baffling breaking ball called the "bat dodger" — made him even more imposing.

Although Paige was banned from playing in the segregated major leagues until 1948, he drew praise from white ballplayers whom he faced in exhibition games. Hall of Fame slugger Joe Dimaggio called him "the best and fastest pitcher I ever faced."

Hall of Fame pitcher Dizzy Dean, another fireballer, said, "Paige is the best pitcher I ever seen, and I been lookin' in the mirror for a long time."

When the Cleveland Indians signed Paige in 1948, he became the oldest rookie in big league history at age 42. He continued to play at different times in the Negro Leagues, big leagues and on barnstorming teams until 1967. Yet Paige never looked at age as a deterrent for playing baseball.

"Age is a question of mind over matter," he once said. "If you don't mind, it doesn't matter."

Paige, a lanky 6-foot-4, 180-pounder with long, wiry arms, was a crowd favorite wherever he went. Fans were "mesmerized by the drama of watching such a remarkable display of audacity and talent by such an unlikely looking source," David Shirley wrote in "Satchel Paige: Baseball Great."

Paige put no limits on himself. When warming up for games, he threw ball after ball over a matchbook, cigarette or bottle top. If he was pitching wild, he'd keep pitching until gaining the accuracy he felt he needed for games, when "I could nip frosting off a cake," he said.

"If you got control, you're going to be pretty hard to hit, because you can find a man's weakness, or your catcher's gonna tell you," he said. "You don't need a curveball or a knuckleball."

Ignored Prejudice

Leroy "Satchel" Paige had humble beginnings. He grew up in a dirt-poor family in segregated Mobile, Ala., where racial slurs were a daily occurrence. But he fought through the prejudice, telling himself that what other people said didn't matter. Instead of listening to them, he focused on his goal: play baseball.

Paige began his love affair with the game when he was 10 and got a job sweeping the grounds at a local baseball stadium. Fascinated, he spent much time watching the games and envisioned himself on the field.

But Paige was too young to play on local teams. Still, he wanted to practice. So he settled for what he thought was the next-best form of molding his talents — throwing rocks at everything in sight.

Case in point: Three chickens once came toward him from 30 feet away. He aimed carefully at the one in the middle, threw a rock and found his mark, killing it and providing food for his family's dinner.

Paige realized he'd found a niche and vowed to stick with it. He aimed at all types of targets from different distances, challenging himself to throw farther and faster each time. He quickly improved his speed, precision and confidence.

"I found out I had control," Paige said. "I could hit about anything with one of those rocks . . . chickens, flying birds. Most people need shotguns to do what I did with those rocks."

He even practiced when he played. While in rock-throwing battles with other kids in the neighborhood, he worked on what later became his "hesitation" pitch. When rival kids ducked behind a tree, he stepped forward to throw but didn't bring his arm around until his left foot came down. That way, kids would peek out and get nailed.

Paige was a mischievous child who constantly tried to push boundaries. He tried to climb higher, run faster than and outwit other children. But in 1918, he went too far. He got caught shoplifting and was committed to a school for troubled kids in Mount Meigs, Ala. It turned out to be a blessing.

The school had a baseball team, and Paige saw an opportunity to realize his dream. He jumped at it.

After making the team, he devoted himself to the game. He watched his opponents carefully to find their weak points. He experimented with different pitches until he found the most effective ones. He listened carefully to coaches and applied their advice when he practiced.

Upon leaving school five years later, he knew he wanted to have a pro baseball career. He didn't just think about it. He went out and chased his dream down.

With blacks barred from the major leagues, he tried out for the Mobile Tigers, an all-black semiprofessional team. He spent two seasons with the squad before breaking into the Negro Leagues in 1926 with the Chattanooga Black Lookouts.

Chattanooga's coach was impressed with the speed of Paige's fastball, but made clear he didn't like his control. Paige got the message. He spent hours and hours improving his control after teammates left the ballpark. He'd line rows of pop bottles across home plate and throw until he knocked them over one after another. Other times, he fired baseballs through a hole no bigger than the inside of a hat lodged in a fence.

Within a year, Paige's control had increased so much that nearly every batter he faced walked to the plate with the fear that he'd strike out.

50

Boxer Rocky Marciano
Total Dedication Helped Him
Land Championships

At 5 feet 10 inches and 185 pounds, Rocky Marciano was one of the smallest heavyweight boxers ever. His short, stubby arms kept him from jabbing at opponents; his reach was a mere 68 inches. By comparison, Muhammad Ali's reach was 82 inches.

How, then, did Marciano become the only world boxing champion to finish his career undefeated at 49-0?

Marciano (1923–69) had the will and strength to take at least half a dozen punches so he could land one. He closed in on foes in a relentless crouching style and threw volleys of punches, overwhelming opponents with powerful shots to the face and body. He often targeted the arms and elbows, weakening them and deflating opponents' ability to throw punches.

Take his sheer determination when he fought Jersey Joe Walcott for the heavyweight championship on Sept. 23, 1952. From the first round, Walcott pounded Marciano with an assortment of devastating shots, sometimes unleashing five in a row.

Blood gushed from a cut above Marciano's eye during one sequence, preventing him from seeing clearly and throwing accurate punches. Walcott knocked him down, too.

The battered Marciano refused to call it quits. But by the end of 12 rounds, Walcott was far ahead on points. The only way for Marciano to win was by a knockout.

Marciano decided to go for it. In the 13th round, he landed a quick left to Walcott's body and followed with his patented right cross that "distorted Walcott's jaw and sent sweat beads of destruction raining from his skull," Everett Skehan wrote in "Rocky Marciano: Biography of a First Son."

Walcott plunged to the canvas and didn't rise for the count. Marciano won the heavyweight crown. It wouldn't have happened if not for his perseverance.

"Most fighters would grab on and wait for their head to clear after being hit by a good combination," boxing referee Ruby Goldstein said. "But this was where Marciano was a discouraging-type fighter. After a fighter hit him with some of his best punches, Rocky would come chasing right after him, back him against the ropes and throw seven or eight punches of his own."

Marciano's victory over Walcott was one of his 43 knockouts, an amazing 26 of which came in the first three rounds. Appropriately, the Brockton, Mass., native was nicknamed the "Brockton Blockbuster." He was inducted into the International Boxing Hall of Fame in 1990.

No Pressure

The kudos that went with his championships didn't turn his head.

In fact, Marciano never let the pressure of boxing matches — or the resultant attention afterward — overwhelm him. He focused on staying calm and relaxed beforehand, taking naps, listening to the radio or joking with friends to remove his mind from the fight. A reporter once said he looked "as nervous as a fire hydrant."

He had humble beginnings. He grew up in Brockton in a poor family during the Great Depression. Money for entertainment was scarce, so he occupied his time by focusing on what he loved doing: playing sports.

He was especially crazy about baseball, and he competed often on the playground. But he never imagined himself being a pro boxer. Actually, it took a lot to provoke him into throwing punches. When fighting, though, he didn't mess around.

"Once Rocky was enraged, he was like an animal," said his friend, Eugene Sylvester. "He really punched the crap out of guys, knocked them right down, blood all over the place. I'd be saying to myself, 'Jeez, why'd I send the Rock after this kid? I've got to be careful who I get him mad at; the Rock's really dangerous.' "

Marciano once got into a fight that ended in a draw. Blood was oozing from his swollen lip. So his uncle, John Picciuto, showed him how to fight properly. Picciuto took an old Army duffel bag, stuffed it with rags and wood shavings and hung it from a tree in the back yard.

Marciano began punching the bag awkwardly. So Picciuto ordered him to use both hands when fighting, yelling "right-left . . . right-left." Marciano listened intently and pummeled the bag that way for hours.

With his uncle's tips in hand, Marciano became a more confident fighter. He also decided that he'd put no limitations on himself in any activity.

"There were guys around Brockton who were bigger and better built than Rock, but they didn't have his determination and guts," said his friend Izzy Gold. "The Rock was always first to take a chance at something we were trying to prove we weren't afraid of. He'd jump a river, climb a tree, swim across a lake, fight a kid three years older than him. I always knew he'd be a winner. He was the kind of kid who wouldn't allow himself to lose."

Marciano realized he'd found his calling with boxing and vowed to stick with it. To become the best possible fighter, he took any advice to heart if he thought it would help him.

Marciano made sure that everything he did — no matter how menial — would help his boxing. Starting in his late teens, he worked various blue-collar jobs. In one, he was "last puller" at a shoe factory. He performed the routine at lightning speed with both hands, pumping up his arms and upper body.

But when Marciano entered the military in 1943, he began smoking two packs of cigarettes a day. When he started fighting amateur bouts in 1946, he was overweight and out of condition. He was exhausted by the third round of his fights.

That was the wake-up call. He told himself that to become a champion boxer, he needed to act like a champion.

So he worked arduously to improve his physical condition. His trainer, Allie Colombo, set up a brutal regimen that included a minimum of seven miles of roadwork per day. Marciano wore heavy training shoes when he ran those miles.

Marciano also ran as fast as he could up a steep incline in Brockton called Tower Hill. He then ambled slowly down the hill and charged right back up, following the routine over and over. Such training was key to his endurance as a pro boxer, especially when he went 15 rounds for the only time in his career against Ezzard Charles in 1954.

To learn to fend off the punches of taller and longer-armed opponents, Marciano practiced throwing fast, accurate passes with a football using both hands. It also helped his powerful jabs, uppercuts and overhand rights.

To achieve peak condition, Marciano knew that every muscle in his body needed to be toned. While other fighters shadowboxed in a ring, Marciano went a step further: He treaded water at the Brockton YMCA as long as he could while throwing underwater punches. He also spent hours and hours working out the old-fashioned way — with the punching bag.

"No one ever got more body weight into a punch when slugging that old YMCA training bag than Rocky Marciano," an onlooker said. "It was obvious to everyone that if he just hit an opponent's arms with those punches, he was going to take the steam out of them. Even way back then, we were absolutely sure he would someday be a world champion."

51

Tennis Powerhouse Serena Williams

She Slammed The Door On The Tennis Competition

In September 2001, tennis held its first Grand Slam final between siblings.

Some billed the U.S. Open duel between Serena Williams and Venus Williams as the biggest match since Bobby Riggs and Billie Jean King's Battle of the Sexes at Houston's Astrodome in 1973.

As the nation tuned in to the prime-time event, a large chorus and Donna Summer rocked New York's Arthur Ashe Stadium. Then Serena and Venus, two of the game's best players, finally entered the court and warmed up.

Did sister rivalry produce a match to remember for years to come? Hardly. It redefined "anticlimactic." Serena Williams sprayed balls wide and long. Elder sis Venus won 6–2, 6–4, but she could barely smile as the sisters embraced at the net.

Serena also had mixed feelings, and who could blame her? Playing against your own kin, the person you practiced with for years and looked up to for advice and inspiration, had to have been painful.

The next year turned out to be different. Serena Williams reflected deeply on how she thought of herself as a tennis player and as a person. She decided it was time to be more independent.

"I thought I liked things (Venus) liked," Williams said after capturing her first Wimbledon crown in 2002. "I realized I didn't like tomatoes. I don't like mushrooms. I had to realize I was a different person. I think this kind of helped."

In January 2003, Serena Williams beat her older sister 7–6 (7–4), 3–6, 6–4 in the final of the Australian Open. Commentators lauded their play as the best between the two.

The victory completed Williams' sweep of all four Grand Slam events, all won against Venus. Only a handful of other women have shown such mastery of all four surfaces, including Maureen Connolly, Margaret Smith Court, Steffi Graf, Chris Evert and Martina Navratilova.

Serena Williams achieved her family's goal of a major championship first, despite expectations that Venus, 15 months older, would be the first.

Serena knocked off world No. 1 Martina Hingis to win the U.S. Open title in 1999. After that breakthrough, however, Serena faded. She suffered injuries and had to pull out of major events such as the Australian Open in 2002. On the long plane ride home, she took stock of her blunders and analyzed each misstep frame by mental frame.

She resolved to stop making easy errors on the court and to get serious about winning the big events.

"Go All Out"

"I didn't have as many distractions in my life, and I made a very big commitment to go all out," she said in a 2003 *Sports Illustrated for Kids* article.

How did Williams mature into a great champion so quickly?

She and her sister started hitting balls with their father and coach Richard before either girl was 6. From the beginning, Serena was greatly inspired by Venus' determination.

"Sixteen years ago, a 4-year-old girl in Compton, Calif., began to cry," Serena wrote in an article on Venus in *Tennis* in January 2001. "She wasn't crying because she lost her doll or because she was hurt. She was crying because her dad wouldn't let her hit all the tennis balls in a grocery cart.

"Her father was teaching her a new sport, and not wanting to overexpose her in one session, he refused to back down. So she started crying, and she refused to stop playing until the basket was empty."

The two young sisters persisted in their dream to become the best in their sport. It wasn't easy, what with their courts amid the tough Los Angeles neighborhood of Compton.

"I think of how hard I worked," Serena said. "People say, 'Oh, you're so lucky to have this.' But luck has nothing to do with it, because I spent many, many hours, countless hours, on the court working for my one moment in time, not knowing when it would come."

Sports psychologists such as Jim Loehr teach tennis players to look at only three things during a match — the ball, the court and the strings. Williams follows the advice and lets nothing faze her.

She also tries to limit stress by not adding extra pressure against herself. Rather than hope or worry about the result, she focuses on hitting the ball well.

At the Australian Open final in January 2003, the first set between the sisters went into a tiebreaker. Any player who has competed in a tournament knows how a tiebreaker alone can be mentally draining.

"You know what? I didn't put any pressure on me. I just went out to play tennis, went out just to do the best that I could do," Williams told a news conference after winning in Melbourne. "I didn't necessarily say, 'I have to do this.' I did often think about, 'OK, I'm only one set away from achieving the accomplishment.'"

Serena and Venus achieved success as junior players. But their father wanted them to avoid the burnout that former stars Tracy Austin and Andrea Jaeger suffered. Austin, who at 14 became the youngest player ever to play Wimbledon, hung up her racket in 1982 at the age of 20. Shoulder injuries forced Jaeger to end her pro career at 18. So he limited the number of events they played each year.

Multitasking

Serena knows she can't play tennis forever. To that end, she designed a line of athletic apparel for Puma and appeared in TV shows while making tennis her full-time job.

Williams has risen to the top by honing the most important stroke in tennis, the serve. It's the only shot in which a player has complete control of the ball. By making it a key strength, she can score many quick points, control the opening exchanges and put extra pressure on opponents when it's their turn to serve.

"Her second serve is better than 95% of the first serves on the women's side," Brad Gilbert, the former pro player, said in a 2003 *Financial Times* article. "And if you don't lose your serve in the women's game, you are never going to lose."

Williams continues to set high goals. She's aiming for an undefeated season. No one in her sport has ever achieved that.

Yet Williams most of all wants to enjoy the game.

During some practices, Williams has been spotted laughing while she tries to return her sister's serves while wearing just one shoe.

"That's just the way she's always been," her sister wrote in the January 2001 issue of *Tennis*.

52

Gymnastics Champ
Nadia Comaneci
Her Drive And Focus Helped
Her Leap To A Perfect 10

For Nadia Comaneci, gymnastics was more than a combination of strength and athletic ability. To win, she felt she had to use all her skills — including brainpower. Before an exercise, Comaneci, a world-class competitor from the mid-1970s to mid-1980s, intently watched the other contestants — and the judges. She watched her opponents' routines and kept an eye on their scores.

Comaneci (pronounced Co-mah-NEECH) would puzzle out what the judges seemed to be doing on a particular day — whether they were emphasizing degree of difficulty or marking down for minor errors.

Then she'd use what she learned. Even though she couldn't make big changes in a carefully planned routine, she could alter subtle points.

While she might make the small changes, Comaneci didn't dwell on her routine during competition. In fact, once she set a goal, she stayed so focused on it that she often couldn't "remember much about my actual performance," she wrote in "Nadia: The Autobiography of Nadia Comaneci." "The only thing I keep close tabs on is the scoring and what I need to achieve in order to win."

Comaneci, who was born in 1961, began learning such focus when she was 3 years old, the age children start kindergarten in her native Romania.

Gymnastics was part of the curriculum, and when she started the sport, the tomboyish Nadia considered it fun. Then famed coach Bela Karolyi spotted her talent. He told her that if she aimed to be the best, she'd need to begin training hard right away. She did, and he eventually took her under his wing.

At 6 years old, Nadia started training with the local gymnastics team, the Flame, which was part of the sports club in Onesti, Romania. Except for eating, she spent every waking hour outside of school practicing.

Two years later she was accepted into the Gymnastics High School, where she spent 4½ hours each day in classes and four more hours training in the gym. In 1970, she was selected to compete in the Romanian National Championships for gymnastics.

Her combination of skill and attitude took her to the top of the gymnastics world. In 1976, at 14 years of age, she won three gold medals and melted hearts across the world during the Montreal Olympics. In 1980, she won two more Olympic gold medals, for a career total of five.

No one was prepared for her outstanding performances in 1976, least of all Olympic and gymnastic officials. No gymnast had ever received a perfect 10-point score, but Comaneci gained 10s in seven exercises. The result was so unexpected that when she won her first 10, the scoreboard gave her mark as 1.0.

Getting Constructive

Although gifted, Comaneci wasn't immediately a perfect competitor. During her first national meet in 1970, she fell from the balance beam three times. She was angry with herself. "I sat alone in my room and brooded," Comaneci wrote.

It didn't last long, however. "I told myself I was never going to be humiliated in such a way again," she said, "and in the future I would take the sport more seriously."

Channeling her anger to a constructive end instead of allowing it to fester is something Comaneci has done all her life: "If I fail to live up to my own standards, I get furious with myself and work twice as hard to compensate. So long as I am not injured in any way, it is an approach that makes sense."

Even at an early age, Comaneci was aware that her gifts alone wouldn't be enough to get to the top. She decided to combine her natural athleticism with discipline and responsibility.

"At times the repetitiveness of training makes concentration and enjoyment difficult to maintain, but you need to keep at it," she said. "A gymnast who does not train seriously does herself a disservice. . . . It is all a question of attitude and self-discipline."

She steadfastly remained confident in herself and her abilities. "I have never worried about names and reputations when competing in gymnastics. In a fair and open event, it does not matter who the opponents are," she'd say.

That's something she learned from Karolyi.

"There is only one thing that counts when it comes to the medals at the competition — who is the best person on that day," he told her. "Don't let anyone's reputation intimidate you. All it means is that they used to be good. They have now got to prove that they still are."

Success meant more than fame and glory for Comaneci. It brought more stress. When the pressure became enormous, she found that physical exercise was a great way to keep on an emotionally even keel.

"If there is something that is (particularly) bugging me, I can work it out of my system by using physical exercise that usually takes the form of gymnastics, but can equally be a brisk swim, a game of tennis, skiing or whatever is going."

Sometimes, however, she's had to recognize when to step away from the pressure. With an infection in her wrist in 1979, Comaneci hadn't been scheduled to compete in a world meet in Fort Worth, Texas. But when a teammate was injured, Karolyi ordered her to do the beam.

"I began my exercise, which became more and more agonizing. By the end, my wrist felt as if it was on fire."

She scored an amazing 9.95 in the event, but had to spend additional time recuperating because she did the routine. She learned a valuable lesson — a goal has to be worth the risk.

Comaneci also wanted others to learn to take care of themselves. "When I coach, I will never expect one of my girls to jeopardize her health in such a way," she said.

The Buck Stops Here

Committed to honesty, Comaneci didn't look for excuses or scapegoats. She preferred to take full responsibility for her actions.

During the 1980 Olympics in Moscow, she fell during her exercise on the uneven bars. That misstep likely cost her Romanian team the gold medal. Afterward, friends rushed to Comaneci's side and offered her an easy way out. They blamed a photographer, the "idiot with the flashgun." But Comaneci wouldn't do that.

"It would have been wonderful to blame somebody else," she said. "I can't remember noticing a bright flash in my eyes during the exercise. . . . The excuse was certainly up for grabs, but I'm afraid it would not have been the truth."

After she stopped competing, Comaneci took a government coaching spot. Because she was a famous athlete, the communist government wouldn't allow her to travel. Languishing in frustration, she realized that freedom was a risk worth taking.

After careful planning, Comaneci and six others walked six hours in cold weather and darkness to cross the border to Hungary in 1989. From there she made her way to the U.S., where she encountered the roughest stretch of her life.

The Romanian expatriate who'd helped her leave Romania had control of her finances. Unsure of herself in a new country, Comaneci believed the man when he threatened to have her sent back if she didn't listen to him.

But old friends from gymnastics came to the rescue, chief among them Bart Conner, an American gymnast and Olympic gold medalist. Comaneci saw the opportunity for real freedom and leapt for it. She began working with Conner to train young gymnasts.

The two married in 1996 and now operate the Bart Conner Gymnastics Academy in Norman, Okla., training a new generation of Olympians.

53

Golf Champ
Jack Nicklaus

His Drive And Focus Swung
Him Into The Record Books

Jack Nicklaus hadn't been on a golf course in nine months in May 1999. He'd gone through hip-replacement surgery just three months earlier. No one would've been surprised if he announced his retirement.

But he was determined to put himself back in the thick of the game he'd loved most of his life.

In a fairy tale, Nicklaus, then 59, would shoot only birdies and eagles, and at the end of the Bell Atlantic Classic in Avondale, Pa., he'd be at the top of the leader board. In reality, he shot 74-70-70. That wasn't bad as the "Golden Bear" approached his golden years, but it wasn't the score legends are made of.

Nicklaus didn't let his loss get to him. Steadfastly optimistic at the tournament's end, he said, "I'm not worried about my golf game. My game will come back."

Yet he refused to look at the caliber of his performance through rose-colored glasses. He recognized that he'd never regain his old strength and flexibility. "The hip is the only thing that works perfectly," he joked at a post-tournament press conference.

Nicklaus' physical limitations didn't mean he approached the tournament with any less dedication than before. "I took myself seriously," he said of his performance. "I need to do that if I'm going to win."

His attitude helped Nicklaus become perhaps the best golfer of all time. He won 20 major tournaments — the Masters, the PGA Championship, the U.S. Open, the British Open and the U.S. Amateur. That's more than anyone else in the history of the game.

Throughout his illustrious career, he won six Masters and four U.S. Opens. He and Walter Hagen won more PGA Championships (five each) than anyone else. He was named Golfer of the Century by two different golf magazines, one American and one British. In the 1970s, *Sports Illustrated* named him Athlete of the Decade.

Eye For Accuracy

Nicklaus began playing golf at just 6 or 7 years old in his hometown of Columbus, Ohio, trailing his pharmacist father, Charlie, around a course.

With an eye for accuracy and a strong swing, Nicklaus' talent soon became apparent. His parents encouraged him to practice hard and challenge himself. He'd often have his father watch him practice and critique his form in an effort to improve.

As he practiced, he'd envision life as a golf professional, winning tournament after tournament. When he made a mistake, he'd refuse to brood about it.

Then he came down with a mild case of polio at age 13. What if he couldn't make his dream come true?

Encouraged by his father and driven by his desire to play golf, Nicklaus fought back with a regimen of strenuous exercise. Every day, he gritted his teeth and plowed through the strength training doctors had given him.

His tenacity helped Nicklaus, at age 13, to become the youngest qualifier for the U.S. Junior Nationals.

He began playing major tournaments in 1957 as an amateur, winning two U.S. Amateur tournaments (1959 and 1961). In 1962, he joined the Professional Golfers' Association Tour and won the first of his four U.S. Open titles.

He continued to visualize success. He mentally walked himself through each course he played on.

All along, Nicklaus relied on the values he'd learned from his father. Charlie taught him responsibility, pride and commitment.

Once, at age 13, Nicklaus was playing nine holes before dinner with his father. Shooting a 35, the younger Nicklaus desperately wanted to keep playing.

Charlie pointed out that he and his son had given their word to Jack's mom, Helen, that they'd be home for dinner. Wanting to teach his son as much about compromise as responsibility, however, Charlie mentioned that if they ate quickly and were polite to Mom, they could be back on the 10th hole in 35 minutes.

Nicklaus learned both lessons well. When designing golf courses today, Nicklaus insists on keeping to schedules. When there's a glitch, however, he looks for a compromise to help the process.

Nicklaus believes integrity is crucial. A few years ago, before the hip replacement, he was participating in an exhibition match sponsored by his course-design company. He admitted his leg was hurting. He gulped down aspirins between holes to ease the pain and did a series of stretching exercises prescribed by his therapist.

The gallery, filled with admiring fans, would have understood if he quit. But he'd made a promise and wanted to honor it.

James Y. Bartlett, a golf writer who volunteered to caddie for Nicklaus that day, wrote in the magazine *Forbes FYI*, "Jack Nicklaus is a proud man. He not only would not give in to the pain, but he refused to let it beat him."

Total Concentration

When he attacks a task, Nicklaus focuses completely on getting it done. Golf pro Phil Rodgers, an old friend, told *Golf Digest* that Nicklaus has the ability "to turn off the rest of the world and concentrate."

Take the end of the 1966 British Open, when Rodgers was paired with Nicklaus.

"I handed him his scorecard. And then he looked at the card he was keeping for me, and he said, 'We have a problem. What did you get on the first hole?' My scorecard was just a blank. He hadn't written down a thing. Effectively, I wasn't there. He had gotten himself into such a state of oneness with the course and concentrated on winning the Open," Rodgers said.

Nicklaus did win — one of his three victories over the years in that event.

Nicklaus leaves his competitiveness on the course and goes out of his way to help friends and colleagues.

"Jack's always been there," former British touring pro Tony Jacklin told *Golf Digest*. "When my wife Vivian died, within three hours of her dying, the phone rang from America, and it was Jack, expressing his disbelief."

Bruce Devlin recalled a time in the early 1960s when he went broke and had to return home to the less competitive New Zealand tour in the hope of winning some tournaments and earning some money. Nicklaus volunteered to house Devlin's wife and children until the family could regroup.

Nicklaus fights for his principles, no matter what. Consider the Casey Martin brouhaha. Martin had a birth defect that required him to use a cart to compete in PGA events. When the PGA refused to grant him an exemption from the rule prohibiting carts at professional golf tournaments, Martin went to court. At the trial, Nicklaus testified against the use of carts.

Asked whether he was concerned about fallout from testifying against Martin, Nicklaus replied: "You're talking about Casey Martin. I'm talking about golf."

Life hasn't all been a breeze for Nicklaus. He's had several business reversals. He lost a reported $12 million in one real estate deal alone. However, he's learned from his mistakes. As he told *Forbes* magazine: "(They) helped me formulate what we have done in the past and what we are going to do in the future."

The proof is Nicklaus' long-term success. Nicklaus' current plate is sprinkled with endorsements for bank, credit card, automobile and apparel companies.

There are also Nicklaus golf clubs and clothing and Nicklaus-designed golf courses (his fee starts at $1.5 million per course).

54

Hockey Player Wayne Gretzky

He Dominated The Ice With Focused Practice And Anticipation

Other hockey players win with brawn. Wayne Gretzky won with brains.

From the time he was a boy, he learned to think about the game. Everybody else chased the puck. Gretzky figured out where it was heading and went to meet it.

He developed his skills on his family's backyard ice rink in Ontario, Canada. His father, Walter, was his coach. He taught him how to turn hockey into a thinking man's sport.

Standing near the center of the rink, Walter would shoot the puck around the boards that bordered the ice and chase behind the puck. After bringing it back, he would shoot it around the boards again. But instead of following behind the puck, he would cut across the rink and intercept it as it came around the boards' rounded corners. The point was not lost on his young son.

"He was teaching me to anticipate," Gretzky said in an interview. "My anticipation, being able to read the play as it is about to unfold, has perhaps been my biggest asset."

At 6 feet and 185 pounds, Gretzky was hardly the biggest or strongest player. Neither was he the fastest or quickest. And "The Great One," as he's been known since he was a child, once claimed his shot couldn't break a pane of glass.

Yet in 1997, a panel of 50 hockey experts ranked Gretzky the No. 1 player in the history of the game. When he retired on April 16, 1999, Gretzky held or shared 61 National Hockey League offensive records. Included are the most career goals (894), most assists (1,963) and most total points — goals and assists combined — 2,857. Seven months after his retirement at age 38, Gretzky was inducted into the NHL Hall of Fame.

Father Knows Best

Gretzky's father was crucial to his development as a player. He had Wayne practicing stickhandling with tennis balls during the summer. The spinning bounce of the tennis balls refined his responses, allowing him to bat flying pucks out of the air with his stick.

That made Gretzky an easy target for the long, airborne clearing passes that create breakaways. And more breakaways meant more goals.

Like his anticipation, Wayne's talent for holding on to the puck can also be traced to that 60-by-40-foot backyard rink built by his father. Walter scattered plastic pylons across the ice, and Wayne wove in and out of the obstacle course while handling the puck.

"All I was trying to do was stick to common sense," Walter said in Terry Jones' "The Great Gretzky." "Pylons work wonders for puck possession."

Despite the repetition, Gretzky never grew bored with the pylon drill. It was that singular focus that allowed him to practice relentlessly.

For instance, when Gretzky was young, he'd skate from 7 to 8:30 a.m., go to school, come home and do his homework, hit the ice again at 3:30 p.m. and skate until his mother called him for dinner.

He'd eat while still wearing his skates. Then he'd go back out and skate until 9 p.m.

"I had a serious addiction to hockey," he admitted in "Gretzky: An Autobiography."

That addiction led to innovation. Gretzky was the first player to use the net regularly to bank passes to teammates when a direct pass wasn't possible.

Sees Everything

Gretzky was also the first to stand behind the net and flip the puck over it off the goalie's back and into the goal. He did it the first time out of necessity. He was trapped behind the net by two defensemen with nowhere to go.

"His awareness is the best of any hockey player I've been around," said John Muckler, who was on the Edmonton Oilers' coaching staff when the team, with Gretzky on it, won four Stanley Cups in the 1980s. He was also the coach for Gretzky's last team, the New York Rangers. "He's always thinking how he can get the advantage."

Gretzky was so plugged in that he saw things on the ice that everyone else missed. He was known to notice that the other team had too many players on the ice when no one else — including the officials — saw it.

Gretzky's potential was apparent early. Most of Canada knew who he was when he was 6. But Gretzky's parents kept him grounded.

"Don't get bigheaded on me," his father would remind him. "No matter how good you are, there's always someone better."

"And I've always remembered that," Gretzky said in his autobiography.

His parents also made sure that hockey wasn't his sole focus. They taught him discipline and showed him what was important — they made him finish his homework before he could play hockey. If you do well in school, his father told him, that focus can help you succeed in sports.

Gretzky, who was an A student, used that discipline to hone his skills year round. In the summer, he'd shoot pucks off steel sheets — which approximated the ice surface — to improve accuracy. When other kids wanted him to go to the movies, he would stay home and practice. His father said he would shoot pucks by himself until it was too dark to see whether they hit the net.

Sometimes he'd "pay friends a nickel or a dime to stay around and play goal against him," Walter said in "Wayne Gretzky: The Making of the Great One."

A Higher Standard

When Gretzky didn't give his full effort, it was his father who pointed out that Gretzky's ability required that he be held to a higher standard than other players.

After the Oilers lost the third game of the 1983 Stanley Cup finals to the New York Islanders, Gretzky put in a poor showing at a practice. Later that summer, the family headed off to visit Gretzky's grandmother, who spent her days working in the garden.

"Look at that. She's 79, and she's still working hard," his father pointed out. "You're 23, and when you're in the Stanley Cup finals, you won't even practice!

"People are going to judge you on how you perform every night. Never forget that."

As Team Canada prepared for the 1987 Canada Cup international tournament, Gretzky found yet another way to improve himself. A young man named Mario Lemieux — thought by many to be the next dominant player — was also on the team. Instead of trying to protect his place as the best, Gretzky taught Lemieux everything he knew, Team Canada coach Mike Keenan said.

"As it turned out, he helped push Mario to another level. But he also pushed himself in the process and sharpened his skills even more," Keenan said in "The Making of the Great One."

Gretzky played 20 seasons in the National Hockey League. His thin body survived all those years of skating in a league of big, strong men who use their size, their sticks, the boards and the ice to punish opponents.

It helped that he played lacrosse, where players hold their sticks at each end and use them to shove their opponents around. Gretzky learned to roll off these crosschecks so he wouldn't be hit straight on.

"It's harder to hit the moving targets than the ones standing still," he said.

To avoid serious injury when a hockey fight broke out — he didn't like it, but it's part of the game — Gretzky searched for an equally small opponent on the ice. Because of his small stature, that man was often equally wary of injury, Gretzky said.

He'd then grab his opponent by the shoulders and hang on as if the two were grappling fiercely, staying clear of more serious fighters. When the fight was broken up, the two separated, usually with no more than a few scrapes.

While the bigger players were cooling their heels, Gretzky was back owning the ice.

55

Football Player
Dan Marino

His Focus Helped Him Climb To The Top Of The Heap

E verything pointed to a milestone football season for Dan Marino. As a senior in 1982 at the University of Pittsburgh, the All-American quarIterback was a preseason favorite to win the Heisman Trophy, college football's premier award. He was designated to lead the Panthers, who were coming off three straight 11-1 seasons, to the national championship.

It never materialized. Marino struggled. Pittsburgh was upset three times to finish with a disappointing 9-3 record. For the first time since he played sports as a child, Marino was the butt of much criticism and frustration.

But Marino didn't sulk. He made the most of his adversity.

"Sports and life are like a roller-coaster ride," he wrote in his autobiography, "First and Goal." "You have to take the ups with the downs. All the struggles and criticism my senior year made me mentally tougher in the long run. Looking back, the season prepared me more for (pro football) than if I had won the Heisman Trophy."

Indeed, Marino's vast mental and physical strengths have shone in the National Football League, where the 17-year veteran was the most proficient passer ever. His NFL records include pass attempts (8,358), completions (4,967), passing yards (61,361) and touchdown passes (420).

How did he do it? By focusing on the skills — namely a strong and accurate throwing arm, a fast release and quick feet — he developed in his youth.

Working It

Marino was born in 1961 and raised in a working-class neighborhood in Pittsburgh. His father, Dan Marino Sr., delivered a Pittsburgh newspaper and was free in the afternoon. They tossed footballs around after school until dusk.

"My dad recognized early that I had a talent for throwing a football, and he always tried to get me to throw with no wasted motion, without dropping the ball, pushing it or winding up," Marino said.

Marino also worked alone on his passing. He'd run down the street with a football, dodging parked cars and throwing the ball at telephone poles, trash cans, street signs and other targets.

His accuracy improved. Friends admired his talents and chose him to quarterback in rough and competitive street football games. He also played street hockey and baseball, getting in as much running as he could.

Football was his first love. He set steep goals for himself, hoping to realize his lifelong dream: becoming a pro football player. Hard work, he thought, would hoist him to that pinnacle.

"If you want to be successful in life, you have to dream," he said. "Once you set your sights on something, you have to go after it with everything you've got. When you give your best effort toward attaining a goal, the odds are in your favor that you'll reach it."

At the same time, Marino had poor grades in middle school. He needed to improve them if he wanted to attend Central Catholic High School, which had long fielded one of Pittsburgh's best sports programs.

His father had often said, "You don't deserve anything in life. You work for what you deserve."

Marino absorbed those words. He worked as hard at his studies as his sports to get into Central Catholic. Once there, he became a multisport star and earned a football scholarship to Pitt.

The best passer in Panther history used the throwing technique he'd developed as a youth and didn't try to emulate anyone. He listened to his coach, Jackie Sherrill, who'd say over and over: "Whatever you do, don't ever let any coach tell you how to throw a football or change anything you're doing. Just keep throwing it the way you do."

But Marino's disappointing senior season lowered his NFL stock. He was the last of six quarterbacks taken in the first round of the 1983 NFL draft, a scenario he found disappointing. Nevertheless, he stayed optimistic about the future with his new team, the Miami Dolphins.

"I made a decision not to be bitter at the teams that passed on me," he wrote. "Instead, I chose to count my blessings and focus my energy on the opportunity at hand."

Marino was true to his word. He had the greatest season for a rookie quarterback ever, posting a 96.0 passing rating, an NFL record to this day. He was also the first rookie quarterback to start in the Pro Bowl, the NFL's all-star game. It launched a brilliant career he spent entirely with the Dolphins.

Power Play

Along the way, Marino developed trademark moves. One of them was an ability to move around in the pocket to constantly avoid the defense's pass rush. The 6-foot-4, 230-pound Marino, who had virtually no scrambling ability, was sacked a total of 69 times, or just 16 times per year.

Knowing that he wanted to develop quicker feet and elude pass rushers, Marino began jumping rope.

Once he spotted a receiver, he deployed his fast throwing motion. The whole sequence was tied to his football instinct, which he developed by directing his mind to analyze a situation immediately.

It's the "ability to feel people around you even though you don't see them," he said. "It comes from doing it your whole life. I have an idea how long a play's going to take if it works right. If something disrupts it, you have a clock ticking in your head that tells you to adjust, to move."

Jim Jensen, a former Marino teammate, said the quarterback had an amazing sense when preparing to throw.

"The amount of time where he sees a target and then his mind tells him to throw, it is a short span," Jensen said. "He sees it, it's gone. There's no thinking."

Marino parlayed his talents into leading the Dolphins to a remarkable 37 comeback wins when they trailed in the fourth quarter. That's when his forward-thinking skills took over.

"During a game, the only thoughts I have are positive," he wrote. "I always say, 'If there's time on the clock, then we're still in the game.' I never think, 'What's going to happen if I miss this throw?' I never think about failure."

Marino knew balance was important. So he complemented his football achievements by being a role model away from the game. His son, Michael, was born with a mild form of autism. So in 1992 he created the Dan Marino Foundation to raise money for children's charities in South Florida. He was named the 1998 NFL Man of the Year, which recognizes player community service and excellence on the field.

"My father always taught me to appreciate what you're fortunate to have and give back to those who need it," Marino said. "No part of our society is more important than the children, especially the ones who need our help."

Despite his fame, Marino remains low-key about his football achievements.

"One of Danny's great traits is he's never lost what he was or where he came from," John Congemi, a Marino friend and former college teammate, once said. "You know exactly where you stand with him — good, bad or indifferent."

Credits

"Baseball Player Willie Mays: He Gave Every Game His All And Became A Legend," by Michael Mink, was originally published in *Investor's Business Daily* on Aug. 23, 2000.

"Mia Hamm Set High Goals: Sure-Footed Competitor Gave America A Leg Up On The Soccer Field," by Michael Mink, was originally published in *Investor's Business Daily* on Nov. 3, 2003.

"Basketball Champ Kareem Abdul-Jabbar: Determination Helped Him Shoot Straight Up," by Kathryn Linderman, was originally published in *Investor's Business Daily* on Aug. 23, 1999.

"Tennis Champ John McEnroe: His Commitment To Perfection Helped Him Win Big," by Curt Schleier, was originally published in *Investor's Business Daily* on July 16, 1999.

"Football Coach Paul 'Bear' Bryant: Determination Drove Him And His Players To Victory," by Michael Mink, was originally published in *Investor's Business Daily* on Oct. 23, 2000.

"Soccer Superstar Pelé: He Became The Game's Greatest By Never Letting His Enthusiasm Flag," by Arthur Goldgaber, was originally published in *Investor's Business Daily* on Oct. 13, 1998.

"Heroic Life Of Ted Williams: Baseball's Last .400 Hitter Swung For Perfection," by Michael Mink, was originally published in *Investor's Business Daily* on July 15, 2002.

"Football Coach Vince Lombardi: His Thirst For Perfection Made His Players Champions," by Steve Watkins, was originally published in *Investor's Business Daily* on June 14, 2000.

"Athlete Babe Didrikson Zaharias: How She Became The Greatest Sportswoman Of Her Time," by Nancy Gondo, was originally published in *Investor's Business Daily* on Sept. 8, 1998.

"Coach George Haines: Innovative And Caring Approach Helped Him Push Swimmers To The Top," by Michael Mink, was originally published in *Investor's Business Daily* on Aug. 1, 2001.

"Harold 'Red' Grange: The Galloping Ghost Helped Rush Pro Football Toward Respectability," by Joannè von Alroth, was originally published in *Investor's Business Daily* on Sept. 8, 2003.

"Blind Climber Erik Weihenmayer: He Faced Down Fear To Reach The Top Of The World," by Peter McKenna, was originally published in *Investor's Business Daily* on June 7, 2001.

"Speed Skater Eric Heiden: Fierce Dedication Helped Him Become An Olympic Champion," by Jonah Keri, was originally published in *Investor's Business Daily* on March 9, 2000.

"Jim Thorpe Earned The Gold: Visualization Pushed Him To Peak Performance," by Brian Deagon, was originally published in *Investor's Business Daily* on Jan. 16, 2002.

"Soccer Great Ronaldo: He Kicked Up His Tenacity To Realize World Cup Goals," by David Saito-Chung, was originally published in *Investor's Business Daily* on July 24, 2002.

"Track Champion Jesse Owens: His Desire And Discipline Made Him A Legend," by Michael Mink, was originally published in *Investor's Business Daily* on Sept. 20, 2000.

"Track Star Wilma Rudolph: Focus And Sheer Grit Won Her Three Olympic Gold Medals," by Lisa Wirthman, was originally published in *Investor's Business Daily* on March 19, 1999.

"Track Champion Carl Lewis: He Kept It Simple To Become One Of The Best," by Michael Mink, was originally published in *Investor's Business Daily* on Sept. 22, 2000.

"Basketball Hall-Of-Famer Jerry West: His Dedication To The Game Made Him An NBA Legend," by Curt Schleier, was originally published in *Investor's Business Daily* on April 26, 1999.

"Golfer Tiger Woods: Constantly Striving To Improve Has Propelled His Career," by Michael Richman, was originally published in *Investor's Business Daily* on March 8, 2000.

"Basketball Player Jackie Stiles: Her Drive For Perfection Helped Make Her The Nation's No. 1 Scorer," by Michael Richman, was originally published in *Investor's Business Daily* on May 9, 2001.

"Iditarod Champ Rick Swenson: His Determination Allowed Him To Glide Ahead Of The Pack," by Amy Reynolds-Alexander, was originally published in *Investor's Business Daily* on Nov. 2, 1999.

"Julius 'Dr. J' Erving: Never Being Satisfied Made Him One Of Basketball's Greatest," by Curt Schleier, was originally published in *Investor's Business Daily* on April 16, 2002.

"Running Back Walter Payton: Determination Helped Him Run Over The Competition," by Chris Warden, was originally published in *Investor's Business Daily* on Nov. 8, 1999.

"Pitcher Nolan Ryan: His Focus Gave Batters 5,714 Reasons To Worry," by Michael Mink, was originally published in *Investor's Business Daily* on Aug. 8, 2001.

"Lance Armstrong Rides To Win: Cycling Champ Races Ahead With Hard Work And Determination," by Amy Reynolds-Alexander, was originally published in *Investor's Business Daily* on Nov. 6, 2001.

"Wrestler And Coach Dan Gable: Hard Work And Focus Helped Make Him The Greatest Wrestler Of The Century," by Sonja Carberry, was originally published in *Investor's Business Daily* on Feb. 15, 2001.

"Babe Ruth Grew To Greatness: Shedding A Poor Childhood, He Became Baseball's Sultan Of Swat," by Michael Mink, was originally published in *Investor's Business Daily* on Aug. 28, 2003.

"Record-Setting Receiver Jerry Rice: His Drive Launched Him Into Football Greatness," by Michael Mink, was originally published in *Investor's Business Daily* on Jan. 24, 2001.

"Tennis Champ Martina Navratilova: Her Resolve To Win Helped Her Make History," by Donna Shew, was originally published in *Investor's Business Daily* on July 2, 1999.

"Jockey Willie Shoemaker: Relentless Determination Helped Put Him In The Lead," by Michael Richman, was originally published in *Investor's Business Daily* on Feb. 1, 2000.

"Heavyweight Boxer Joe Louis: Unwavering Discipline Made Him Longest-Reigning Champ," by Kerry Jackson, was originally published in *Investor's Business Daily* on Dec. 6, 1999.

"Swimming Champ Mark Spitz: Drive For Excellence Made Him The Best," by Michael Mink, was originally published in *Investor's Business Daily* on July 6, 2001.

"Basketball Coach John Wooden: Careful Analysis Helped Him Scale The Pyramid Of Success," by Michael Mink, was originally published in *Investor's Business Daily* on March 29, 2000.

"Runner Roger Bannister: He Broke The Four-Minute Mile, Proving There Are No Limits," by Ira Breskin, was originally published in *Investor's Business Daily* on May 20, 1998.

"Baseball Player Jackie Robinson: Dedication Helped Him Become A Legend," by Michael Mink, was originally published in *Investor's Business Daily* on Oct. 12, 2000.

"Tennis Player Althea Gibson: She Made Her Hits Count," by Michael Mink, was originally published in *Investor's Business Daily* on Oct. 2, 2003.

"Basketball Coach Phil Jackson: Focus On Teamwork Took His Players To The Top," by Michael Mink, was originally published in *Investor's Business Daily* on Jan. 4, 2000.

"Boxer Muhammad Ali: Dedication And Innovation Helped Make Him A Champion," by J. Barnes, was originally published in *Investor's Business Daily* on Aug. 4, 2000.

"Baseball Executive Branch Rickey: His Vision And Courage Integrated The Game," by Michael Mink, was originally published in *Investor's Business Daily* on Sept. 14, 2000.

"Skating Champ Peggy Fleming: Perseverance Helped Her Jump To The Gold," by Curt Schleier, was originally published in *Investor's Business Daily* on Oct. 4, 1999.

"Ivan Lendl's Grand Tennis Rise: He Slammed His Way To No. 1 With Mental and Physical Preparation," by Michael Mink, was originally published in *Investor's Business Daily* on Dec. 31, 2003.

"Driver Michael Schumacher: He Races To Win," by Adelia Cellini Linecker, was originally published in *Investor's Business Daily* on June 7, 2002.

"Basketball Coach 'Red' Auerbach: He Shot For The Best To Make Sure His Team Came Out On Top," by Daniel J. Murphy, was originally published in *Investor's Business Daily* on Sept. 24, 1999.

"Triathlete Paula Newby-Fraser: She Became The Best By Keeping Her Mind Clear," by Amy Reynolds-Alexander, was originally published in *Investor's Business Daily* on May 25, 1999.

"Golf Champ Nancy Lopez: Focus And Positive Attitude Helped Her Win Championships And Fans' Hearts," by Sarah Z. Sleeper, was originally published in *Investor's Business Daily* on July 30, 2001.

"Sprinter Florence Griffith Joyner: She Trained Her Mind As Hard As She Did Her Body," by Michael Richman, was originally published in *Investor's Business Daily* on Sept. 28, 1998.

"Basketball Legend Michael Jordan: Discipline And Desire Made Him Synonymous With Success," by Michael Mink, was originally published in *Investor's Business Daily* on Nov. 12, 2001.

"Baseball Great Satchel Paige: Focus Kept Him Aiming High," by Michael Richman, was originally published in *Investor's Business Daily* on Sept. 24, 2001.

"Boxer Rocky Marciano: Total Dedication Helped Him Land Championships," by Michael Richman, was originally published in *Investor's Business Daily* on Sept. 7, 2001.

"Tennis Powerhouse Serena Williams: She Slammed The Door On The Tennis Competition," by David Saito-Chung, was originally published in *Investor's Business Daily* on March 26, 2003.

"Gymnastics Champ Nadia Comaneci: Her Drive And Focus Helped Her Leap To A Perfect 10," by Curt Schleier, was originally published in *Investor's Business Daily* on Sept. 21, 2000.

"Golf Champ Jack Nicklaus: His Drive And Focus Swung Him Into The Record Books," by Curt Schleier, was originally published in *Investor's Business Daily* on Oct. 18, 2000.

"Hockey Player Wayne Gretzky: He Dominated The Ice With Focused Practice And Anticipation," by Kerry Jackson, was originally published in *Investor's Business Daily* on Sept. 21, 1998.

"Football Player Dan Marino: His Focus Helped Him Get To The Top Of The Heap," by Michael Richman, was originally published in *Investor's Business Daily* on Jan. 31, 2000.

Index

About *Investor's Business Daily*

Investor's Business Daily provides critical, no-nonsense finance and investing information to nearly a million readers every day. Known for its innovative approach and straightforward analysis, it's one of today's most essential tools for empowering individual and institutional investors. Visit online at www.investors.com.